A practical introduction to denotational semantics

Also in this series

1 An Introduction to Logical Design of Digital Circuits
C. M. Reeves 1972

2 Information Representation and Manipulation in a Computer
E. S. Page and L. B. Wilson, Second Edition 1978

3 Computer Simulation of Continuous Systems
R. J. Ord-Smith and J. Stephenson 1975

4 Macro Processors
A. J. Cole, Second Edition 1981

5 An Introduction to the Uses of Computers
Murray Laver 1976

6 Computing Systems Hardware
M. Wells 1976

7 An Introduction to the Study of Programming Languages
D. W. Barron 1977

8 ALGOL 68 – A first and second course
A. D. McGettrick 1978

9 An Introduction to Computational Combinatorics
E. S. Page and L. B. Wilson 1979

10 Computers and Social Change
Murray Laver 1980

11 The Definition of Programming Languages
A. D. McGettrick 1980

12 Programming via Pascal
J. S. Rohl and H. J. Barrett 1980

13 Program Verification using Ada
A. D. McGettrick 1982

14 Simulation Techniques for Discrete Event Systems
I. Mitrani 1982

15 Information Representation and Manipulation using Pascal
E. S. Page and L. B. Wilson 1983

16 Writing Pascal Programs
J. S. Rohl 1983

17 An Introduction to APL
S. Pommier 1983

18 Computer Mathematics
D. J. Cooke and H. E. Bez 1984

19 Recursion via Pascal
J. S. Rohl 1984

20 Text Processing
A. Colin Day 1984

21 Introduction to Computer Systems
Brian Molinari 1985

22 Program Construction
R. G. Stone and D. J. Cooke 1986

23 Cambridge Computer Science Texts

A practical introduction to denotational semantics

Lloyd Allison

Department of Computer Science, University of Western Australia

CAMBRIDGE
UNIVERSITY PRESS

Published by the Press Syndicate of the University of Cambridge
The Pitt Building, Trumpington Street, Cambridge CB2 1RP
40 West 20th Street, New York, NY 10011-4211 USA
10 Stamford Road, Oakleigh, Melbourne 3166, Australia

First published 1986
Reprinted 1995

British Library cataloguing in publication data

Allison, Lloyd
A practical introduction to denotational semantics. – (Cambridge computer science text)

1. Programming languages (Electronic computers) – Syntax 2. Programming languages (Electronic computers) – Semantics
I. Title
005.13 QA76.7

Library of Congress cataloguing in publication data

Allison, Lloyd.
A practical introduction to denotational semantics.

(Cambridge computer science texts; 23)
Bibliography
Includes indexes.
1. Programming languages (Electronic computers) – Semantics. I. Title. II. Series.
QA76.7.A45 1987 005.13 86-12961

ISBN 0 521 30689 2 hard covers
ISBN 0 521 31423 2 paperback

Transferred to digital printing 2003

MP

Contents

Preface

This is an introductory textbook on denotational semantics intended for interested computer scientists, for undergraduates towards the end of their course and for postgraduates beginning theirs. The material has been used in a final-year undergraduate course at the University of Western Australia for some years. The objective is to introduce readers to the range of material, both mathematical and practical, in the subject so that they may carry out simple applications and understand more advanced material.

The mathematical foundations of denotational semantics are covered in sufficient detail to illustrate the fundamental problems in semantic theory that were solved by Scott. The section is self-contained but a background including a computer-science or mathematics course on discrete structures or algebra would be helpful. It can be skipped on a first reading or omitted by a reader prepared to take the foundations on trust.

The remainder of the book covers the use of denotational semantics to describe sequential programming languages. Knowledge of at least one high-level programming language, such as Ada, Algol, C, Modula, Pascal or PL1, is essential. It is an advantage to be aware of the general features of several languages so as to realize the variety available. Familiarity with compilation, interpretation and functional programming is also a help.

A great deal of emphasis is placed on practical work. The usual notation of denotational semantics is akin to a powerful functional programming language. In fact it is somewhat arbitrary and a denotational definition can be expressed in a variety of programming languages and can be compiled and run to give an implementation. I believe that the best way to learn the subject is to practise it, to write definitions. Few tests of a language definition are as rigorous as submitting it to a compiler for type checking and then running. The best programming language in which to write a denotational definition is a (semantic) compiler-compiler or a typed functional language such as ML. Quite a lot can be done with Algol-68 and Pascal which are available on a wide range of computers and, where appropriate, definitions are translated into these languages in the text.

Writing and running such a definition, or modifying an existing one, makes an excellent exercise or project. This culminates in an executable semantics of the core of the logic-programming language Prolog which can form the basis of experiments on different semantics for different versions of Prolog.

This being an introduction, not all of denotational semantics is covered. Those wishing to discover more of the mathematical foundations should read Stoy [58]; to see more techniques for describing programming languages read Milne and Strachey [36] (2 vols). Tennent [62] gives an excellent short introduction to denotational semantics. For an alternative view of the subject see Gordon [21]. Pagan [48] and McGettrick [35] survey several semantic formalisms. References to the research literature are given throughout the book.

Acknowledgements

This book does not extend the theory of denotational semantics but draws on the work of D. Scott, C. Strachey, R. Milne and C. Wadsworth. It is also influenced by the work of M. Gordon, F. Pagan, J. Stoy, R. Tennent and many others.

I would like to thank Jeff Rohl for encouraging me to write the book, Robin Milner and Alan Mycroft for discussing type systems with me, Rodney Topor and an anonymous referee for making suggestions to improve the text and Chris McDonald and Trevor Dix for help with word processing. Any errors are, of course, all my own.

R: Exp →... right values
T: Texp →...
U unify
V: Num → Int
Y: ((T→T) → T→T) → T→T fixed-point operator
| alternation (or) in grammar rules
∀ for all
∃ there exists
⊆ subset
⊇ superset
∪ union
∩ intersection
: membership of set or data type
→ function type
× multiplication, direct product
∘ functional composition
⇒ implies
⇐ implied by
:– Prolog implied by or 'if'
⊢ as in P⊢Q, Q can be deduced from P in some proof system
∨ disjunction, or
∧ conjunction, and
~ negation, not
⊥ bottom, undefined element
⊤ top, overdefined element
⟦ ⟧ semantic brackets
{ } enclose continuations
⟨ ⟩ enclose tuples
⊑ less defined, approximates
⊒ more defined, approximated by
⊔ least upper bound

Glossary

Principal uses of the Greek letters and other special characters:

α alpha	Prolog atom
β beta	beta-conversion
γ gamma	command
δ delta	declaration (and Prolog database)
ε epsilon	expression
ζ zeta	Prolog location
η eta	eta-conversion
θ theta	command continuation
κ kappa	expression kontinuation (*sic*)
λ lambda	lambda-abstraction
μ mu	fixed-point operator
ν nu	numeral, constant
ξ xi	identifier
π pi	Prolog predicate
ρ rho	environment
σ sigma	store, also state
τ tau	type expression
ϕ phi	label
χ chi	declaration continuation
ψ psi	Prolog query
Λ Lambda	type abstraction
Ξ Xi	Prolog variable identifier
Ω Omega	binary operator
C: Cmd $\to$...	direct semantics
D: Dec $\to$...	
E: Exp $\to$...	
L: Exp $\to$...	left values
O: Opr $\to$...	operators
P: Cmd $\to$...	continuation semantics
Q: Query $\to$...	Prolog

1 Introduction

Denotational semantics is a formal method for defining the semantics of programming languages. It is of interest to the language designer, compiler writer and programmer. These individuals have different criteria for judging such a method – it should be concise, unambiguous, open to mathematical analysis, mechanically checkable, executable and readable depending on your point of view. Denotational semantics cannot be all things to all people but it is one attempt to satisfy these various aims. It is a formal method because it is based on well-understood mathematical foundations and uses a rigorously defined notation or meta-language.

The complete definition of a programming language is divided into *syntax*, *semantics* and sometimes also *pragmatics*. Syntax defines the structure of legal sentences in the language. Semantics gives the meaning of these sentences. Pragmatics covers the use of an implementation of a language and will not be mentioned further.

In the case of syntax, context-free grammars expressed in Backus–Naur form (*BNF*) or in syntax diagrams have been of great benefit to computer scientists since Backus and Naur [44] formally specified the syntax of Algol-60. Now all programming languages have their syntax given in this way. The result has been 'cleaner' syntax, improved parsing methods, parser-generators and better language manuals. As yet no semantic formalism has achieved such popularity and the semantics of a new language is almost invariably given in natural language.

The typical problem facing a programmer is to write a program which will transform data satisfying some properties or assertions 'P' into results satisfying 'Q'.

$$\{P\} \text{ program } \{Q\}$$

The language of the assertions is predicate logic. This formulation treats a program as a predicate transformer.

Concentrating on the predicates in the transformation leads to the *axiomatic* style of semantics. This was suggested by Floyd [17] and formalized and developed by Hoare [24], Dijkstra [13] and many others. The method is readable and very useful to programmers and designers of algorithms. It is intimately connected with the discipline of structured programming. It has, not insurmountable, difficulties in defining some features of programming languages, notably **gotos** and side-effects in expressions. There is heated debate, not to be taken up here, as to whether this is a drawback of the method or an indication that these features are hard to use and dangerous. Note that interest in predicate logic has created the programming language Prolog [9] (Ch 9).

Concentrating on the program as a function mapping inputs satisfying P into results satisfying Q leads to *operational* and denotational semantics. Operational semantics imagines the program running on an abstract machine. The machine may be quite unlike any real computer, either low-level, simple and easy to analyse, or high-level with an easy translation from the programming language. The machine and the translation must be specified. Such a definition is most useful to a compiler writer if the abstract machine is close to the real hardware. To be useful mathematically it may require quite different properties.

Denotational semantics recognizes the subtle distinction between a function as a probably infinite set of ordered pairs $\{\langle input_i, output_i\rangle\}$ and an algorithm as a finite description of the function. A program is the algorithm written in some particular programming language. A program stands for, or denotes, a function. A denotational semantics of a programming language gives the mapping from programs in the language to the functions *denoted*.

Example

factorial $= \{\langle 0,1\rangle, \langle 1,1\rangle, \langle 2,2\rangle, \langle 3,6\rangle, \langle 4,24\rangle, \ldots\}$
fact(n) $=$ if n$=$0 then 1 else n $\times$ fact(n $-$ 1)

A good semantics should confirm that program fact denotes the factorial function.

Denotational semantics is written in *λ-notation* which is the λ-calculus of Church [7] with data-types. It has a well-developed mathematical theory and the foundations have been thoroughly investigated. The method is concise and powerful enough to describe the features of current programming languages. Mosses [40] gives a definition of Algol-60 and Tennent [63] gives one for Pascal, for example. Such definitions are only readable with practice, the notation being equivalent to a powerful but terse programming language. It is more suitable for the language designer and implementor than the programmer.

McCarthy [34] based the programming language Lisp on the λ-calculus, and other languages, particularly in the Algol family, show a similar influence. Lisp was perhaps the first programming language designed on mathematical semantic principles. Much of the motivation for the wider application of denotational semantics to all programming languages came from Strachey [59, 60]. Scott [54, 55, 56] solved many of the mathematical problems raised concerning the existence and consistency of objects defined in a semantics. One benefit of denotational semantics is that it can be 'mechanized'. Mosses' SIS [41] is an interpreter for denotational semantics that enables a definition to be run – used to execute programs in the defined language. Paulson's compiler-compiler [49] translates a definition into a compiler. Certain functional programming languages such as ML [20] are very close to the typed λ-notation and can be used to write, and run, denotational definitions.

It seems that an axiomatic definition and a denotational definition make good partners; the former for the programmer, the latter for the language designer. The theme of Donahue's book [14] is that such definitions can be shown to be consistent with each other and he does this for a large subset of Pascal.

Note that denotational semantics is part of a wide movement including model theory in logic, philosophy and linguistics. For example, Montague semantics [15] attempts to give a denotational style of semantics for a subset of English. Logicians are concerned with the objects that names, variables and predicates stand for and with what it means for a statement to be true.

This introduction has omitted much, in particular extensions of grammars to include semantics. *Attribute grammars* associate attribute evaluation functions with grammar rules. These can be used operationally to evaluate to code, or denotationally to evaluate to functions. *Two-level grammars* [65] are also powerful enough to specify the input–output behaviour of programs [8].

In the remainder of the book, after some motivating examples, there is an introduction to the λ-notation, data-types and the mathematical foundations of denotational semantics. This is followed by applications to the definition of programming-language features. The notation of even denotational semantics is somewhat arbitrary (!) and throughout it is shown how definitions can be programmed in conventional languages and executed.

1.1 An example

To give the flavour of denotational semantics, the classic example of decimal numerals follows. Decimal numerals form a language, **Num**, over the *alphabet* $\{0,1,2,3,4,5,6,7,8,9\}$. It can be defined by the *grammar*

$$\nu ::= \nu\delta \mid \delta$$
$$\delta ::= 0|1|2|3|4|5|6|7|8|9$$

The symbol '::=' can be read as 'is' or 'can be replaced by'. The '|' can be read as 'or'. A digit δ is a 0 or a 1 or a 2 and so on. A numeral ν is a numeral followed by a digit or it is a single digit. The Greek letters δ and ν are syntactic variables over parts of the language **Num**.

The decimal numerals are usually taken to stand for, or taken to *denote*, integers which are abstract objects. This conventional interpretation can be made formal by giving a valuation function **V**:

$$\mathbf{V}: \mathbf{Num} \to \mathbf{Int}$$
$$\mathbf{V}[\![\nu\delta]\!] = \mathit{10} \times \mathbf{V}[\![\nu]\!] + \mathbf{V}[\![\delta]\!]$$
$$\mathbf{V}[\![0]\!] = \mathit{0} \quad \mathbf{V}[\![1]\!] = \mathit{1}$$
$$\mathbf{V}[\![2]\!] = \mathit{2} \quad \mathbf{V}[\![3]\!] = \mathit{3}$$
$$\mathbf{V}[\![4]\!] = \mathit{4} \quad \mathbf{V}[\![5]\!] = \mathit{5}$$
$$\mathbf{V}[\![6]\!] = \mathit{6} \quad \mathbf{V}[\![7]\!] = \mathit{7}$$
$$\mathbf{V}[\![8]\!] = \mathit{8} \quad \mathbf{V}[\![9]\!] = \mathit{9}$$

V is a function from the sentences in the language **Num** to the integers **Int**. **V** is defined on a case-by-case analysis of the alternatives in the grammar for **Num**. Elements of the language are enclosed in the special brackets $[\![$ and $]\!]$ to distinguish them from the meta-language outside. Inside the brackets are strings. The integers outside the brackets are in *italics*. 7 is a character which denotes the integer *7*. It is impossible to write anything down without using names and so we are forced to adopt some such convention.

The value of a particular numeral can now be calculated:

$$\mathbf{V}[\![123]\!] = \mathit{10} \times \mathbf{V}[\![12]\!] + \mathit{3}$$
$$= \mathit{10} \times (\mathit{10} \times \mathbf{V}[\![1]\!] + \mathit{2}) + \mathit{3}$$
$$= \mathit{123}$$

This may prompt the reaction 'so what, isn't that obvious?' The reply is that we should be pleased that the formal definition agrees with intuition in simple cases. This is a feature of good theories. The formalism is needed when intuition is not strong enough. The reader who does not realize that the statement 7 = '7' is not only not true, but is an error in Pascal, may have missed the point. Note that **V** has captured the essence of positional notation, and that $\mathbf{V}[\![123]\!] = \mathbf{V}[\![0123]\!]$ and so on.

The definition of **V** can be used to design a piece of code that exists in most compilers:

```
if ch in ['0'..'9'] then
begin n := ord(ch) - ord('0');
      ch := nextch {return next char and advance input↑};
      while ch in ['0'..'9'] do
      begin n := n*10 + ord(ch) - ord('0');
            ch := nextch
      end
end
```

Numerals that occur in a program must have their values calculated by the compiler.

In what follows the languages examined will be more interesting and the things they are mapped onto will be more complex. The general scheme, however, is always to map a language onto a collection of abstract objects.

1.2 Exercises

1. If the first case in the definition of **V** is changed to

   $\mathbf{V}[\![\nu\delta]\!] = -10 \times \mathbf{V}[\![\nu]\!] + \mathbf{V}[\![\delta]\!]$

   what are the new characteristics of **V**? What advantage does this new interpretation of **Num** have?

2. Give a grammar and a semantic valuation function for roman numerals made up of I (one), V (five) and X (ten) only. It will be simpler to have a grammar which allows unusual but comprehensible numerals such as

   IIIII five
   IIIIIV zero
   VV ten

   although

   IVX

   should not be allowed as it is ambiguous – four or six.

   To include the full range of roman numerals L (fifty), C (hundred), D (five hundred), M (thousand), follows a similar pattern and just makes the solution larger.

2
Basics

This chapter introduces basic notation for syntax and semantics by examples. As such, some ideas are used before their (proper) definition; however, what is going on should be intuitively clear.

2.1 Abstract syntax

It is usual to distinguish between the *concrete syntax* and the *abstract syntax* of a programming language. Concrete syntax defines the way the language is actually written on paper or on a screen and includes sufficient information to parse it. Abstract syntax specifies the relations between logical parts of the language; it can be simpler and may not contain enough information to parse the language unambiguously. Denotational semantics is usually based on the simpler more fundamental abstract syntax although this is not essential.

As an example, an **if** command might have the following concrete syntax:

$$\gamma ::= \textbf{if}\ \varepsilon\ \textbf{then}\ \gamma\ \textbf{else}\ \gamma\ \textbf{fi}$$

But the abstract syntax might be given as

$$\gamma ::= \textbf{if}\ \varepsilon\ \textbf{then}\ \gamma\ \textbf{else}\ \gamma$$

or even

$$\gamma ::= \varepsilon \rightarrow \gamma, \gamma$$

which emphasizes that the essential components are a controlling expression and two subcommands. (γ is the syntactic variable for commands.)

The concrete syntax of an expression might be

$$\varepsilon ::= \varepsilon + \tau \mid \tau$$
$$\tau ::= \tau \times \psi \mid \psi$$
$$\psi ::= (\varepsilon) \mid \mathrm{a} \mid \mathrm{b} \mid \mathrm{c} \mid \ldots$$

This specifies that $\mathrm{a}+\mathrm{b}\times\mathrm{c}$ should be parsed as $\mathrm{a}+(\mathrm{b}\times\mathrm{c})$ and not as $(\mathrm{a}+\mathrm{b})\times\mathrm{c}$. The sequence of rules gives the operators $+$, $\times$ and ( ) in increasing order of priority or binding strength. This information might be lost in the abstract syntax

Exp:
$\varepsilon ::= \varepsilon + \varepsilon |$
$\quad \varepsilon \times \varepsilon |$
$\quad a | b | c | \ldots$

which only specifies the crucial information that an expression is either an operand or an operator applied to two subexpressions. It is an ambiguous grammar and would allow a + b × c to be parsed in either way if used for that purpose. The parentheses ( ) need not appear as they only serve to control parsing.

At a practical level, concrete syntax can be used to code a recursive-descent parser:

```
procedure exp;
   procedure term;
      procedure opd;
      begin {opd}
         if ch='('
            then {sub-exp}
               begin insymbol {set sy to next symbol};
                     exp;
                     check([')']) {call insymbol if sy in set, else error}
               end
            else check(['a'..'z'])
      end;
   begin {term}
      opd;
      while ch='×' do
      begin insymbol;
            opd
      end
   end;
begin {exp}
   term;
   while ch='+' do
   begin insymbol;
         term
   end
end
```

The abstract syntax can define a data structure, or parse tree, that might be produced by a parser:

```
type expntype=(opd, plus, times);
     expn=↑node;
     node=record cast t:expntype of
                    opd:(id:ch);
                    plus, times:
                         (left, right:expn)
          end
```

Semantic definitions are usually based on abstract syntax. It is assumed that somewhere concrete syntax exists and that a parser can analyse programs correctly. The result of the parser corresponds to the abstract syntax and the denotational definitions are given in terms of it.

2.2 Sequential execution

It is obvious that numerals most sensibly stand for numbers. The objects that programs denote are more complex. It is common to think of a program transforming a state, as in Ch 1, with every assignment.

A *state* defines the current values of the variable identifiers in the program:

$$\mathbf{S} = \mathbf{Ide} \rightarrow \mathbf{Value}$$

States, **S**, is the set or data-type of functions from identifiers, **Ide**, to **Value**. A particular state

$$\sigma{:}\mathbf{S}$$

is a particular function from variables to values. The colon ':' indicates that σ is in the data-type **S**. Suppose $\sigma[\![x]\!]=6$ and $\sigma[\![y]\!]=9$ then with an abuse of axiomatic notation we might write

$$\{\sigma\}\ x := x+1\ \{\sigma'\}$$

where

$$\sigma'[\![x]\!]=7, \quad \sigma'[\![y]\!]=9.$$

(All of the predicates that hold before the assignment can be inferred from σ and all of those that hold afterwards can be inferred from σ'.)

A command denotes a state transformation in

$$\mathbf{S} \rightarrow \mathbf{S}$$

The valuation function for commands, **C**, maps commands onto state transformations:

$$\mathbf{C}{:}\ \mathbf{Cmd} \rightarrow (\mathbf{S} \rightarrow \mathbf{S})$$

$\rightarrow$ is defined to associate to the right so this is usually written

$$\mathbf{C}: \mathbf{Cmd} \rightarrow \mathbf{S} \rightarrow \mathbf{S}$$

A command, γ:**Cmd**, denotes the state transformation

$$\mathbf{C}[\![\gamma]\!]: \mathbf{S} \rightarrow \mathbf{S}$$

Given the example above,

$$\mathbf{C}[\![\mathrm{x} := \mathrm{x}+1]\!]\sigma = \sigma'$$

Note that parentheses, for example around σ, are omitted wherever possible, and that function application is left-associative:

$$\mathrm{f\,x\,y} \equiv (\mathrm{f(x)})(\mathrm{y})$$

A central feature, one of the most important characteristics of a large number of programming languages including Basic, Cobol, Fortran and Pascal is sequential execution. A program is executed by executing the first command then the second one and so on – assuming the absence of jumps which are dealt with in Ch 7. All these languages contain sequences of commands. The following abstract syntax defines this, although it is most closely based on Pascal.

Cmd:

$\gamma ::= \gamma;\ \gamma | \ldots$

The ';' in Pascal can be read as 'and then'. Execute command one and then execute command two.

A command of the form $\gamma_1;\gamma_2$ denotes the state transformation

$$\mathbf{C}[\![\gamma_2]\!] \circ \mathbf{C}[\![\gamma_1]\!]$$

where $\circ$ is functional *composition*. Note the order; $(\mathrm{f} \circ \mathrm{g})(\mathrm{x}) = \mathrm{f}(\mathrm{g}(\mathrm{x}))$.

Example Given $\sigma[\![\mathrm{x}]\!] = 6$, $\sigma[\![\mathrm{y}]\!] = 9$

$$\begin{aligned}
&\mathbf{C}[\![\mathrm{x} := \mathrm{x}+1;\ \mathrm{y} := \mathrm{x}]\!]\sigma \\
&= \mathbf{C}[\![\mathrm{y} := \mathrm{x}]\!] \circ \mathbf{C}[\![\mathrm{x} := \mathrm{x}+1]\!]\sigma \\
&= \mathbf{C}[\![\mathrm{y} := \mathrm{x}]\!]\sigma' \\
&= \sigma''
\end{aligned}$$

where $\sigma''[\![\mathrm{x}]\!] = \sigma''[\![\mathrm{y}]\!] = 7$.

To extend the abstract syntax to include compound statements or commands, add

Cmd:

$\gamma ::= \mathbf{begin}\ \gamma\ \mathbf{end}\ | \gamma;\ \gamma | \ldots$

$$\mathbf{C}[\![\mathbf{begin}\ \gamma\ \mathbf{end}]\!] = \mathbf{C}[\![\gamma]\!]$$

Using the fact that functional composition is associative, the following three program schemes can be shown equivalent:

(1) $\gamma 1;\ \gamma 2;\ \gamma 3$

(2) **begin** $\gamma 1;\ \gamma 2$ **end**; $\gamma 3$

(3) $\gamma 1$; **begin** $\gamma 2;\ \gamma 3$ **end**

This is as it should be and increases confidence that the definition of **C** is correct as far as it goes.

The definition of the valuation function **C** can be given in many notations. It cannot be translated directly into standard Pascal for reasons addressed later, but the following is very close:

```
function C(g: cmd; s: State): State;
   ...
   case g↑.tag of
      semicolon: C := C(g↑.right, C(g↑.left, s))
      ...
   end
```

The second command, g↑.right, is applied to the result of the first command, g↑.left.

2.3 Expressions

The class of expressions in a programming language varies from language to language but must include at least boolean expressions for control commands.

Exp:

$\varepsilon ::= \varepsilon$ **and** ε |
ε **or** ε |
not ε |
true |
false |
ξ

Ide:

ξ ::= syntax for identifiers

E: Exp → S → Bool

$\mathbf{E}[\![\varepsilon \textbf{ and } \varepsilon']\!]\sigma = \mathbf{E}[\![\varepsilon]\!]\sigma \wedge \mathbf{E}[\![\varepsilon']\!]\sigma$

$\mathbf{E}[\![\varepsilon \textbf{ or } \varepsilon']\!]\sigma = \mathbf{E}[\![\varepsilon]\!]\sigma \vee \mathbf{E}[\![\varepsilon']\!]\sigma$

$\mathbf{E}[\![\textbf{not } \varepsilon]\!]\sigma = \sim \mathbf{E}[\![\varepsilon]\!]\sigma$

$\mathbf{E}[\![\textbf{true}]\!]\sigma = \mathit{true}$

$\mathbf{E}[\![\textbf{false}]\!]\sigma = \mathit{false}$

$\mathbf{E}[\![\xi]\!]\sigma = \sigma[\![\xi]\!]$

The value denoted by an expression depends on the state because it may contain variables. **E** maps an expression onto a function from states to values, here just boolean values. For a particular expression, ε, $\mathbf{E}[\![\varepsilon]\!]$: $\mathbf{S} \to \mathbf{Bool}$ is a function from **S** to **Bool**, $\mathbf{E}[\![\varepsilon]\!]\sigma$: **Bool**. This definition of **E** assumes that expressions do not have side-effects that might alter the state. This will be allowed later.

2.4 Control commands

An **if** command can be added to the syntax of commands by

Cmd:
$\gamma ::= \mathbf{if}\ \varepsilon\ \mathbf{then}\ \gamma\ \mathbf{else}\ \gamma \mid \ldots$

Its semantics is given by

$$\begin{aligned}&\mathbf{C}[\![\mathbf{if}\ \varepsilon\ \mathbf{then}\ \gamma\ \mathbf{else}\ \gamma']\!]\sigma\\ &= \mathbf{C}[\![\gamma]\!]\sigma \quad \text{if } \mathbf{E}[\![\varepsilon]\!]\sigma = \mathit{true}\\ &= \mathbf{C}[\![\gamma']\!]\sigma \quad \text{otherwise}\end{aligned}$$

A special function Cond is defined

$$\begin{aligned}&\mathrm{Cond}\colon (\mathbf{S} \to \mathbf{S})^2 \to \mathbf{Bool} \to (\mathbf{S} \to \mathbf{S})\\ &\mathrm{Cond}(\mathrm{p}, \mathrm{q})\mathit{true} = \mathrm{p}\\ &\mathrm{Cond}(\mathrm{p}, \mathrm{q})\mathit{false} = \mathrm{q}\end{aligned}$$

Cond takes two state transformations p and q, and produces a function from a boolean switch to a state transformation. If the switch is *true* Cond picks the first transformation, otherwise the second.

$$\begin{aligned}&\mathbf{C}[\![\mathbf{if}\ \varepsilon\ \mathbf{then}\ \gamma\ \mathbf{else}\ \gamma']\!]\sigma\\ &= \mathrm{Cond}(\mathbf{C}[\![\gamma]\!], \mathbf{C}[\![\gamma']\!])(\mathbf{E}[\![\varepsilon]\!]\sigma)\sigma\end{aligned}$$

It is worth examining this to make sure that the types all match.

$$\begin{aligned}&\mathbf{C}\colon \mathbf{Cmd} \to \mathbf{S} \to \mathbf{S}\\ &\mathbf{C}[\![\mathbf{if} \ldots]\!]\colon \mathbf{S} \to \mathbf{S}\\ &\mathbf{C}[\![\mathbf{if} \ldots]\!]\sigma\colon \mathbf{S}\\ &\mathrm{Cond}(\mathbf{C}[\![\gamma]\!], \mathbf{C}[\![\gamma']\!])\colon \mathbf{Bool} \to \mathbf{S} \to \mathbf{S}\\ &\mathbf{E}[\![\varepsilon]\!]\colon \mathbf{S} \to \mathbf{Bool}\\ &\mathbf{E}[\![\varepsilon]\!]\sigma\colon \mathbf{Bool}\\ &\mathrm{Cond}(\ldots)(\mathbf{E}[\![\varepsilon]\!]\sigma)\colon \mathbf{S} \to \mathbf{S}\\ &\mathrm{Cond}(\ldots)(\mathbf{E}[\![\varepsilon]\!]\sigma)\sigma\colon \mathbf{S}\end{aligned}$$

The equation using Cond is rather hard to read so it is often written in the more convenient infix style

$$\begin{aligned}&\mathbf{C}[\![\mathbf{if}\ \varepsilon\ \mathbf{then}\ \gamma\ \mathbf{else}\ \gamma']\!]\sigma\\ &= (\text{if } \mathbf{E}[\![\varepsilon]\!]\sigma \text{ then } \mathbf{C}[\![\gamma]\!] \text{ else } \mathbf{C}[\![\gamma']\!])\sigma\end{aligned}$$

but the **if** inside the brackets $[\![\ ]\!]$ is part of the language being defined and the 'if' outside them is part of the meta-language. Note, it is important that the definition is not given as

$$\text{Cond}(\mathbf{C}[\![\gamma]\!]\sigma, \mathbf{C}[\![\gamma']\!]\sigma)(\mathbf{E}[\![\varepsilon]\!]\sigma)$$

or

$$\text{if } \mathbf{E}[\![\varepsilon]\!]\sigma \text{ then } \mathbf{C}[\![\gamma]\!]\sigma \text{ else } \mathbf{C}[\![\gamma']\!]\sigma$$

This poor definition implies that the two commands are executed to produce two alternative states and one of these is picked depending on the result of the expression. The original definition says use the result of the expression to pick one of the state transformations denoted by the two commands and execute that one only. Note also that an alternative specification of Cond would be needed in the second definition to make the types match.

A **while** command can be defined syntactically as:

Cmd:

$\gamma ::= \textbf{while } \varepsilon \textbf{ do } \gamma \mid \ldots$

The result of

$$\mathbf{C}[\![\textbf{while } \varepsilon \textbf{ do } \gamma]\!]\sigma$$

depends on $\mathbf{E}[\![\varepsilon]\!]\sigma$. If it is *false*, σ is unchanged. The result is just σ or $\text{Id}(\sigma)$ where $\text{Id}:\mathbf{S} \to \mathbf{S}$ is the identity function. If the result of the expression is *true* the result is

$$\mathbf{C}[\![\textbf{while } \varepsilon \textbf{ do } \gamma]\!] \circ \mathbf{C}[\![\gamma]\!]\sigma$$

that is, apply γ to σ and do the loop again. In summary,

$$\mathbf{C}[\![\textbf{while } \varepsilon \textbf{ do } \gamma]\!]\sigma$$
$$= \text{Cond}(\mathbf{C}[\![\textbf{while } \varepsilon \textbf{ do } \gamma]\!] \circ \mathbf{C}[\![\gamma]\!], \text{Id})(\mathbf{E}[\![\varepsilon]\!]\sigma)\sigma$$

or equivalently

$$= (\text{if } \mathbf{E}[\![\varepsilon]\!]\sigma \text{ then } \mathbf{C}[\![\textbf{while } \varepsilon \textbf{ do } \gamma]\!] \circ \mathbf{C}[\![\gamma]\!] \text{ else Id})\sigma$$

This is a recursive definition in that the meaning of a **while** loop depends upon itself. This is potentially troublesome because this sort of equation can have zero, one, a few or even infinitely many solutions! Naturally a programming language's semantics should have exactly one solution or meaning. Recursive definitions are examined in the chapter on mathematical foundations, Ch 4.

2.5 Exercises

1. Take the manual of your favourite programming language and turn to its syntax definition in BNF or syntax diagrams. Indicate how these rules for

concrete syntax could be collapsed and simplified into (an) abstract syntax.

2. Show that

if ε
  then begin γ_1; γ_2 **end**
  else begin γ_3; γ_2 **end**

and

begin if ε **then** γ_1 **else** γ_3 **end;** γ_2

are equivalent for arbitrary γ_1, γ_2 and γ_3 by application of the rules for **C** and **E**.

3
λ-Notation

λ-Notation is the meta-language of denotational semantics. It is based on the λ-calculus with the addition of types. Lisp [34] and other programming languages have been influenced by the λ-calculus which can claim to be the prototype functional programming language. It is Church's [7] *thesis*, since it cannot be proven, that λ-calculus captures exactly those functions that can be computed by mechanical or electronic means. Since other notions of computation such as the Turing machine have been shown to be equivalent to it, this is widely accepted. λ-Calculus allows us to write λ-expressions and to manipulate them formally. A λ-expression denotes a function but often, to be concise, it is identified with the function. Firstly basic types or domains are examined. Following the untyped λ-calculus, the typed and the polymorphic λ-calculi are defined.

3.1 Domains

For the time being, the existence of certain elementary *domains* is assumed; their exact structure, which turns out to be that of a lattice (Ch 4), is examined later:

Int the domain of integers
Char the domain of character values
Bool the domain of truth values
true: **Bool**, *false:* **Bool**†

For the moment, a domain can be thought of as a set.

The *direct product* of domains A and B, A × B, is the domain of ordered pairs:

$\{\langle a, b\rangle | a: A \text{ and } b: B\}$

There are associated *projection* functions from A × B to A, written $\langle a, b\rangle_1 = a$ or $\langle a, b\rangle[1] = a$, and from A × B to B written $\langle a, b\rangle_2 = b$ or

† It might be more strictly correct to write **true:Bool** and *true* ∈ *Bool* where ∈ is set membership, but the distinction will not be made here.

$\langle a, b\rangle[2]=b$. As a shorthand, $A \times A$ is written A^2, and so on for higher powers. If A is an alphabet of characters, $\langle a, a'\rangle$ is often written as aa'. The special case $A^0=\{\langle\ \rangle\}$ is the domain of the empty ordered tuple or the empty word.

The *union* of domains A and B, $A \cup B$, is the domain of elements that are either in A or in B:

$$A \cup B=\{x \mid x: A \text{ or } x: B\}$$

The domain of all strings, ordered tuples or words of *finite* length over an *alphabet* A is:

$$\begin{aligned} A^* &= A^0 \cup A^1 \cup A^2 \cup \ldots \\ &= \bigcup_{i \geqslant 0} A^i \end{aligned}$$

The members of A^* are of finite length, for $s: A^*$ only if $s: A^i$ for some i and i must be finite – although there is no limit on what i may be. The domain of all non-empty strings over A is:

$$A^+=A^1 \cup A^2 \cup \ldots$$

The *disjoint union* or *disjoint sum* of domains A and B, $A+B$, is

$$\{\langle a, 1\rangle \mid a: A\} \cup \{\langle b, 2\rangle \mid b: B\}$$

There are membership testing functions from $A+B$ to **Bool**:

$$\begin{aligned} &\text{isA}\langle a, 1\rangle=\text{isB}\langle b, 2\rangle=\textit{true} \\ &\text{isA}\langle b, 2\rangle=\text{isB}\langle a, 1\rangle=\textit{false} \end{aligned}$$

The injection functions from A to $A+B$ and from B to $A+B$,

$$\begin{aligned} &\text{in}_1(a)=\langle a, 1\rangle: A+B \\ &\text{in}_2(b)=\langle b, 2\rangle: A+B \end{aligned}$$

are often implicit. If $x: A+B$ and $x=\langle a, 1\rangle$, the projection onto $x_1=a$ is usually implicit.

If A and B are disjoint, there is a one-to-one correspondence between members of $A \cup B$ and of $A+B$ by mapping a onto $\langle a, 1\rangle$ and b onto $\langle b, 2\rangle$. In that case notation is sometimes abused and $A \cup B$ and $A+B$ may be treated as equivalent.

For the time being, these definitions can be thought of as the traditional set-theoretic operations. Later, the resulting domains will be seen to have the same lattice structure referred to above.

These operations have been taken up by various programming

languages and can be expressed in Pascal, say:

```
type axb=record x: a; y: b end;
     aplusb=record case t: onetwo of
                        1: (x: a);
                        2: (y: b)
            end
```

Pascal supports a restricted **set** data-type. Strings and sequences can be programmed by linked lists or by files.

3.1.1 *Functions*

A *relation* from domain A to domain B is a subset of A × B. If A = B we talk of a (binary) relation on A.

Example

States = {Vic, SA, NSW, Qld, NT, WA, Tas}
Borders = {⟨Vic, NSW⟩, ⟨Vic, SA⟩,
⟨NSW, Qld⟩, ⟨NSW, SA⟩, ⟨NSW, Vic⟩,
⟨WA, SA⟩, ⟨WA, NT⟩,
⟨SA, WA⟩, ⟨SA, NT⟩, ⟨SA, Qld⟩, ⟨SA, NSW⟩, ⟨SA, Vic⟩,
⟨Qld, NT⟩, ⟨Qld, SA⟩, ⟨Qld, NSW⟩,
⟨NT, WA⟩, ⟨NT, SA⟩, ⟨NT, Qld⟩}

Borders is a relation on the states of Australia.

A *partial function* f from A to B is a relation from A to B such that for each a: A there is at most one b: B for which ⟨a, b⟩: f. A *total function* f from A to B is a relation from A to B such that for each a: A there is exactly one b: B for which ⟨a, b⟩: f.

Example

factorial = {⟨*0*, *1*⟩, ⟨*1*, *1*⟩, ⟨*2*, *2*⟩, ⟨*3*, *6*⟩, ...}

Factorial is a partial function from **Int** to **Int** but it is a total function from the non-negative integers to **Int**. Note that Borders is neither a total nor a partial function from States to States.

This definition of function may appear strange to programmers. What Pascal calls a **function** is something quite different, in fact an algorithm, a finite description of a method for calculating a function.

It is common practice to write f(a) = b rather than ⟨a, b⟩: f. If 'op' is a function from A × B to C, the following are all equivalent:

$\langle a, b, c\rangle : op$
$op(\langle a, b\rangle) = c$ prefix
$a \; op \; b = c$ infix

In this case op is called a binary operator.

A function from A to B is *one-to-one* (*1-1*) if $f(a_1) = f(a_2)$ implies that $a_1 = a_2$. f is *onto* if for all b: B there is some a: A such that $f(a) = b$. If f is total, 1-1 and onto then the *inverse function* f^{-1} defined by

$$f^{-1}(b) = a \text{ where } f(a) = b$$

is indeed a function and is total and 1-1 from B onto A.

Functional *composition*, o, is defined by

$$(f \circ g)(x) = f(g(x))$$

If f is a total, 1-1 and onto function from A to B then $f \circ f^{-1}$ is the identity function on B and $f^{-1} \circ f$ is the identity function on A.

It is often necessary to produce new *updated* functions from old ones. f[v/x] is a new function derived from f by updating f with a new value v at x:

$$\begin{aligned} f[v/x](y) &= v && \text{if } y = x \\ &= f(y) && \text{otherwise} \end{aligned}$$

Note that f is not altered in any way; f[v/x] is a new function closely related to f but quite distinct from it.

The domain of functions from A to B is written $A \to B$. It turns out to have the most interesting structure of all the derived domains. For the time being, exactly which functions are allowed to be in $A \to B$ is left unspecified. Note that $\to$ associates to the right so that

$$A \to B \to C = A \to (B \to C)$$

$A \to B$ is close to **function**(A): B in Pascal, except that **function** is not part of the Pascal type system. The Algol-68 **proc(A)B** is closer.

3.2 Untyped λ-calculus

Church's *λ-calculus* [7] is a formal system for the study of functions, their definition and application. Devised before electronic computers, it has a claim to be the archetypal functional programming language.

The basic λ-calculus is very economical, not to say sparse. Its syntax is:

$$\begin{aligned} \varepsilon ::= & \; \varepsilon\,\varepsilon && | \text{ application} \\ & \lambda\xi . \varepsilon && | \text{ abstraction} \\ & \xi && | \text{ variable} \\ & (\varepsilon) \end{aligned}$$

If x is a variable identifier, plus(x, sqr(x)) or in more convenient notation, $x+x^2$, is an expression in which x is *free*. A free variable must either be defined globally to the expression or be undefined. If x is somehow associated with a value, 7 say, then $x+x^2$ is equivalent to 56. The expression

$$\lambda x . x+x^2$$

is an *abstraction* of $x+x^2$. The x is *bound* by the λx. This is the definition of an anonymous function with x as formal parameter. There is no equivalent in Pascal but in Algol-68, omitting the **modes**, one could write

proc(x): x + sqr(x)

For convenience the definition of named expressions is allowed but this is not strictly necessary. For now, named expressions must be defined before use, prohibiting explicit recursion.

Examples

$Id = \lambda x . x$ identity function

$k = \lambda x . (\lambda y . x)$

As a further shorthand, local definitions in the style

ε where $\xi = \varepsilon$

or

let $\xi = \varepsilon$ in ε

are also allowed.

3.2.1 *Conversion*

Manipulation of λ-expressions is governed by the rules of *conversion*. Taken together these define function application or call and a scope rule for bound variables equivalent to that of block-structured languages like Pascal.

Substitution of an expression 'e' for an identifier 'x' is straightforward except where name clashes could arise:

$$\varepsilon\varepsilon'[e/x] = (\varepsilon[e/x])(\varepsilon'[e/x])$$

$$\lambda\xi . \varepsilon[e/x] = \lambda\xi . \varepsilon \quad \text{if } \xi = x \qquad (2)$$

$$= \lambda\xi' . (\varepsilon[\xi'/\xi][e/x]) \quad \text{if } \xi \neq x, \text{ x free in } \varepsilon \text{ and } \xi \text{ free in e, } \xi' \text{ a new var} \qquad (3)$$

$$= \lambda\xi . (\varepsilon[e/x]) \quad \text{otherwise}$$

$$\xi[e/x] = e \quad \text{if } \xi = x \quad \text{(substitute for the var)}$$

$$= \xi \quad \text{otherwise}$$

$$(\varepsilon)[e/x] = (\varepsilon[e/x])$$

Line (2) above indicates that local bindings take priority and defines the scope-rule. Line (3) prevents name clashes between $\lambda\xi.\varepsilon$ and e, for example:

$$\lambda x.(x+y^2)[(x+1)/y] = \lambda u.u+(x+1)^2$$

α-Conversion allows the systematic renaming of formal parameters:

$$\alpha :- \quad \text{if y is not free in } \varepsilon, \quad \lambda x.\varepsilon \equiv \lambda y.\varepsilon[y/x]$$

This should be quite familiar to any programmer; parameter names are 'dummy' names and can be changed 'consistently'. y must not be free in ε to prevent variable *capture*.

Examples

$\lambda x.x = \lambda y.y$

$\lambda x.\lambda x.x = \lambda x.\lambda y.y$

But

$\lambda x.\lambda y.x \neq \lambda x.\lambda x.x$

would be capture by [y/x].

β-Conversion is the rule for function application. It defines the substitution of an actual parameter for the formal parameter. It is textual substitution as in a macro-processor.

$$\beta :- \quad ((\lambda x.\varepsilon)a) \equiv \varepsilon[a/x]$$

Examples

$(\lambda x.\text{plus}(1,x))7 = \text{plus}(1,7)$

$(\lambda x.x)(\lambda y.y) = \lambda y.y$

$(\lambda x.(\lambda x.x))7 = \lambda x.x$

The application of β-conversion from left to right simplifies an expression and is called *β-reduction.*

An optional third rule, η-conversion, allows any expression to be treated as a function

$$\eta :- \quad \varepsilon \equiv \lambda x.\varepsilon x$$

provided that x is not free in ε, to prevent variable capture. An application of η-conversion from right to left simplifies an expression and is called an η-reduction.

3.2.2 *Evaluation*

The conversion rules allow λ-expressions to be reduced or evaluated. An expression that cannot be reduced further is in *normal form* and this can be taken to be the result of the expression. Unfortunately not all expressions have a normal form, for example:

$$(\lambda x\,.\,xx)(\lambda y\,.\,yy) = (\lambda y\,.\,yy)(\lambda y\,.\,yy) = (\lambda x\,.\,xx)(\lambda y\,.\,yy)$$

Although there is no definition of named functions in pure λ-calculus, and therefore no recursion in the Pascal sense, the above example clearly has a recursive or self-applicative nature.

There may also be a choice in the order that rules are applied in when reducing an expression.

$$(\lambda x\,.\,y)((\lambda x\,.\,xx)(\lambda y\,.\,yy))$$

gives the choice of applying β-reduction to either $(\lambda x\,.\,y)(\ldots)$ or $((\lambda x\,.\,xx)(\lambda y\,.\,yy))$. The first choice gives just

$$y$$

which is in normal form. The second choice gives the original expression; if this is repeated we get an infinite loop.

Fortunately it is not possible for two different sequences of reductions to terminate while returning different results. Either they both terminate in equivalent normal forms up to α-conversion or at least one does not terminate. Furthermore, a special order of evaluation called *normal order* always terminates if any one will and so has a claim to be the most general evaluation rule. It involves always applying the left-most outermost β-reduction possible. These results are due to Church and Rosser.

Normal-order evaluation corresponds to passing parameters *by-name* which is an option in Algol-60, or to textual substitution as in a macro-processor, because the evaluation of an actual parameter is deferred until its use in a function. In the example above the actual parameter's evaluation is deferred forever. The outermost driving function is always 'run' first and its parameters are evaluated as and when it needs them, if at all. In contrast, many programming languages such as Pascal pass parameters *by-value* by default, in which case they are evaluated *before* being passed to the function.

3.2.3 *Constants*

Despite the economy of λ-calculus it is possible to define λ-expressions that behave like the integers and the standard operations on them. Supposing that there were a function to give zero, z, and a successor function, s, then the non-negative integers would be represented by:

$$z,\quad s(z),\quad s(s(z)),\quad \ldots$$

Therefore it is adequate to use:

$\lambda s.\lambda z.z$ zero
$\lambda s.\lambda z.s(z)$ one
$\lambda s.\lambda z.s(s(z))$ two
...

Addition of a and b can be coded as:

$$\text{plus} = \lambda a.\lambda b.\lambda s.\lambda z.a\,s\,(b\,s\,z)$$

plus one two
$= \lambda s.\lambda z.\text{one}\;s(\text{two}\;s\;z)$
$= \lambda s.\lambda z.(\lambda z.s\,z)(s(s\,z))$
$= \lambda s.\lambda z.s(s(s\,z))$
$=$ three

It is common, however, to add some constants to the λ-calculus, typically to stand for the integers and integer operations but perhaps standing for more complex objects, such as lists, structures and functions, depending on the application:

$\varepsilon ::= \varepsilon\,\varepsilon$ |
$\lambda\xi.\varepsilon$ |
ξ |
(ε) |
ν constants

For each constant there must be reduction rules for its correct use, including error conditions.

3.2.4 *High-order functions*

It is quite natural for a function to produce a function as a result or to have a function as a parameter. Such functions are *high-order* functions.

Examples

$(\lambda x.\lambda y.x)7 = (\lambda y.7)$

so

$(\lambda x.\lambda y.x)7\;3 = (\lambda y.7)3 = 7$

$\text{twice} = \lambda f.\lambda x.f(f\,x)$
$\text{succ} = \lambda x.x+1$

twice succ
$= \lambda x.(\lambda x.x+1)((\lambda x.x+1)x)$
$= \lambda x.((\lambda x.x+1)x)+1$
$= \lambda x.x+1+1$
$= \lambda x.x+2$

twice accepts a function f as its parameter and produces a function which is the composition of f with itself. Note that the abbreviations

$$\text{let } \xi = \varepsilon \text{ in } \varepsilon'$$

and

$$\varepsilon' \text{ where } \xi = \varepsilon$$

are equivalent to

$$(\lambda\xi \,.\, \varepsilon')\varepsilon$$

As a shorthand, $\lambda x \,.\, \lambda y \,.\, e$ may be written $\lambda x, y \,.\, e$.

A function of two parameters can be represented as a function with one parameter which is a pair:

$$\text{swap} = \lambda x \,.\, \langle x_2, x_1 \rangle$$
$$\text{swap}\langle 1, 2 \rangle = \langle 2, 1 \rangle$$

A *pattern-matching* form is allowed for convenience:

$$\text{swap} = \lambda\langle x, y \rangle . \langle y, x \rangle$$

or

$$\text{swap}\langle x, y \rangle = \langle y, x \rangle$$

For any function of two parameters, there is a corresponding higher-order function.

$$f = \lambda\langle x, y \rangle . e$$
$$f' = \lambda x, y \,.\, e$$

f and f′ are related by

$$f\langle x, y \rangle = f' \, x \, y \quad \forall x \text{ and } y$$

f′ is called the *curried* version of f after Curry although he [12] attributes the technique to Schonfinkel. It is possible to define currying and uncurrying functions:

$$\text{curry} = \lambda f \,.\, \lambda x, y \,.\, f\langle x, y \rangle$$
$$\text{uncurry} = \lambda f \,.\, \lambda\langle x, y \rangle . fxy$$

so that curry(f) = f′ and uncurry(f′) = f. One advantage of f′ over f is that f′(x) is defined but f(x, ?) is not. A proposed extension to Algol-68 called *partial parameterization* allowed for definitions like fx = f(x,) after which fx(y) = f(x, y).

Standard stack-based languages such as Pascal do not allow curried functions to be written, but an extension called Functional Pascal [19] does:

```
function twice(function f: intfn):
        function(x: integer): integer;
begin twice := f(f(x)) end
```

This can be used as in

function plus2 = twice(succ)

and then plus2(4) = twice(succ)(4) = 6.

The closest that can be achieved in Pascal is to use uncurried twice:

function utwice(**function** f(i: integer): integer;
x: integer): integer;
begin utwice := f(f(x)) **end**

and then utwice(succ, 4) = 6.

Some high-order functions have already been used:

$o = \lambda\langle f, g\rangle . \lambda x . f(g(x))$ composition
Cond: $(\mathbf{S} \to \mathbf{S})^2 \to \mathbf{Bool} \to \mathbf{S} \to \mathbf{S}$

3.3 Recursion

The functions expressed in λ-calculus so far have not used self-reference or *recursion*. Indeed, the definition of named functions is only a shorthand and is not strictly necessary; definition was required before use, forbidding self-reference. In fact explicit self-reference is not necessary to code recursion in λ-calculus!

Here the desired effects of recursive definitions are investigated. Experts in a recursive programming language must do some forgetting and try to recall the surprise that a novice experiences when getting to grips with recursion.

Given the definition

$y = x + 1$

x is free and so y is unknown. Given the definitions

$x = 7$
$y = x + 1$

clearly y = 8. Given

$x = 7$
$y = f(x)$

f is free and y is unknown, but given

$x = 7$
$f = \lambda z . z + 1$
$y = f(x)$

then y = 8 again. Note that, if x is free in e,

$x = z$
$y = e$

defines y to be the same as

$$y=(\lambda x\,.\,e)z$$

What is required in a recursive definition is the ability to write

$$f=e$$

where f is free and occurs in e, for example

$$\text{when}\quad f=\text{fact},\ e=\lambda x\,.\,\text{if } x=0 \text{ then } 1 \text{ else } x\times f(x-1)$$
$$\text{fact}=\lambda x\,.\,\text{if } x=0 \text{ then } 1 \text{ else } x\times \text{fact}(x-1)$$

This is to have one's cake and eat it, to use fact before it is defined and this may not be valid. The aim is to get the effect of the infinite expression

$$f=(\lambda f.e)((\lambda f.e)((\lambda f.e)\ldots))$$

or of the infinite sequence of definitions

$$\begin{aligned}&\ldots\\ &f_{i+1}=(\lambda f\,.\,e)(f_{i+2})\\ &f_i=(\lambda f\,.\,e)(f_{i+1})\\ &\ldots\\ &f_2=(\lambda f\,.\,e)(f_3)\\ &f_1=(\lambda f\,.\,e)(f_2)\\ &f=f_1\end{aligned}$$

and it must be shown that this is reasonable.

Recall that given

$$g=\lambda x\,.\,\text{if } x=0 \text{ then } 1 \text{ else } x\times f(x-1)$$
$$y=g(7)$$

g and y are undefined because f is free. Given

$$f=\text{succ}$$
$$g=\lambda x\,.\,\text{if } x=0 \text{ then } 1 \text{ else } x\times f(x-1)$$
$$y=g(7)$$

then $y=7\times \text{succ}(7-1)=49$. This is equivalent to

$$g=\lambda f\,.\,\lambda x\,.\,\text{if } x=0 \text{ then } 1 \text{ else } x\times f(x-1)$$
$$y=g\ \text{succ}\ 7$$

The intention of the recursive definition of 'fact' is to set up an *equation* which hopefully has a solution, 'the' factorial function, and that this is what fact should be defined as.

If F is defined as

$$F=\lambda f\,.\,\lambda x\,.\,\text{if } x=0 \text{ then } 1 \text{ else } x\times f(x-1)$$

the recursive definition previously given is seeking a *fixed point* of F, because it is fixed or unchanged by F. If factorial is the 'real' factorial function then

F factorial
$= \lambda x\,.\,\text{if } x=0 \text{ then } 1 \text{ else } x \times \text{factorial}(x-1)$
$=$ factorial

so factorial is certainly *a* fixed point of F.

Unfortunately an equation of this sort can have zero, one, a few or even infinitely many solutions. Consider

$x = x + 1$
$x = 7$
$x = 9/x$
$x = x$

If any recursive definitions appear in the semantics of a programming language, as is almost certain, it is important that they each have exactly one natural solution so that the language is defined and well defined. The example, fact, actually has infinitely many solutions! For any fixed point f of F, f(x) is determined for all $x \geqslant 0$ but

$f(-1) = -1 \times f(-2)$
$f(-2) = -2 \times f(-3)$

and so on. An entirely arbitrary choice can be made for $f(-1)$ and this fixes the other results of f on negative arguments. The lattice theory examined later removes this ambiguity in a natural way and ensures that there is only one meaning attached to programs like

```
function fact(x: integer): integer;
begin if x=0
          then fact := 1
          else fact := x × fact(x − 1)
end
```

3.3.1 *Fixed-point operator* Y

It is possible to define an operator, **Y**, in the λ-calculus that finds fixed points if they exist. This means that recursive functions can be coded without explicitly recursive definitions, even without any definitions at all! Such a **Y** must have the property that

$$\mathbf{Y}F = F(\mathbf{Y}F)$$

for any suitable high-order function F. One definition of **Y** is

$$\mathbf{Y} = \lambda G\,.\,(\lambda g\,.\,G(gg))(\lambda g\,.\,G(gg))$$

then

$$\begin{aligned}
&\mathbf{YF}\\
&= (\lambda G\,.\,(\lambda g\,.\,G(gg))(\lambda g\,.\,G(gg)))\ F\\
&= (\lambda g\,.\,F(gg))(\lambda g\,.\,F(gg)) && (3)\\
&= F(\ (\lambda g\,.\,F(gg))(\lambda g\,.\,F(gg))\ )\\
&= F(\text{line}(3))\\
&= F(\mathbf{YF})
\end{aligned}$$

so **YF** really is a fixed point of F.

Example

$$\mathbf{F} = \lambda f\,.\,\lambda x\,.\,\text{if } x=0 \text{ then } 1 \text{ else } x \times f(x-1)$$

$$\begin{aligned}
&\mathbf{YF}\\
&= (\lambda G\,.\,(\lambda g\,.\,G(gg))(\lambda g\,.\,G(gg)))(\lambda f, x\,.\,\text{if } x=0 \text{ then } 1 \text{ else } x \times f(x-1))\\
&= (\lambda g\,.\,(\lambda f, x\,.\,\text{if } x=0 \text{ then } 1 \text{ else } x \times f(x-1))(gg))(\text{ditto})\\
&= (\lambda f, x\,.\,\text{if } x=0 \text{ then } 1 \text{ else } x \times f(x-1))\\
&\qquad ((\lambda g\,.\,(\lambda f, x\,.\,\text{if } x=0 \text{ then } 1 \text{ else } x \times f(x-1))(gg))\\
&\qquad (\text{- - - - - - - - - - ,, - - - - - - - - - ,, - - - - - - - - - -}))\\
&= (\lambda x\,.\,\text{if } x=0 \text{ then } 1 \text{ else}\\
&\qquad x \times ((\lambda g\,.\,(\lambda f, x\,.\,\text{if } x=0 \text{ then } 1 \text{ else } x \times f(x-1))(gg))\\
&\qquad\quad (\text{- - - - - - - - - - ,, - - - - - - - - - ,, - - - - - - - - - -}))(x-1)\\
&= \lambda x\,.\,\text{if } x=0 \text{ then } 1 \text{ else } x \times \mathbf{YF}(x-1)
\end{aligned}$$

Y is called the *paradoxical operator* or combinator, possibly because of its relevance to self-referential paradoxes, or possibly because its workings are subtle and paradoxical! **Y** applied to F builds an expression which contains a copy of **YF**. This expression can be applied to an argument and may immediately produce a result, as in ⟨*0, 1*⟩. *0!* = *1*. In this case the copy **YF** is never applied. Otherwise, **YF** is applied to x − 1 and so on. **YF** is substituted inside F, or unwound, just enough times for a result to be produced. This is what the recursive definition of 'fact' (§ 3.3) intended. **Y** does not magically prevent a recursive expression from looping, as **YF**(−1) will show.

Note that **Y** allows anonymous recursive functions to be defined:

$$\mathbf{Y}(\lambda f, x\,.\,\text{if } x=0 \text{ then } 1 \text{ else } x \times f(x-1))$$

is an expression for the anonymous factorial function.

It is possible to code **Y** and F in Algol-68 by uncurrying them.

```
mode rect = proc(rect, int)int
     intfn = proc(int)int,
     fform = proc(intfn, int)int;

fform F = (intfn f, int x)int:
  if x = 0 then 1 else x × f(x − 1) fi;

proc Y = (fform G, int n)int:
  (rect p = (rect g, int m)int:
     (intfn q = (int n)int: g(g, n); c q ≡ gg c
      G(q, n)   c ≡ G(gg)n c
     );
   p(p, n)
  )
 Y(F, n) ≡ n!
```

Note that this requires a recursive type or **mode**, **rect**, see also §3.4 and §8.2.2. It is not possible to code **Y** in Pascal because **function** is not part of the type system, but it can easily be coded in Functional Pascal.

3.4 Typed λ-calculus

The simply typed λ-calculus is the λ-calculus as before with the addition of simple types.

$$\begin{aligned} \varepsilon ::= \; & \varepsilon\,\varepsilon \mid \\ & \lambda\xi : \tau\,.\,\varepsilon : \tau \mid \\ & \xi \mid \\ & \nu \mid \\ & (\varepsilon) \end{aligned}$$

Texp:

$$\begin{aligned} \tau ::= \; & \mathbf{Int} \mid \mathbf{Bool} \mid \ldots \mid \\ & \tau \times \tau \mid \tau + \tau \mid \tau \to \tau \end{aligned}$$

Examples

$\mathrm{succ} = \lambda x : \mathbf{Int}\,.\,x + 1 : \mathbf{Int}$

$\mathrm{id}_{\mathbf{Int}} = \lambda x : \mathbf{Int}\,.\,x$

$\mathrm{id}_{\mathbf{Bool}} = \lambda x : \mathbf{Bool}\,.\,x$

A type may be omitted if it is obvious from context.

There are type-checking rules for expressions:

$$\varepsilon : \tau \to \tau' \text{ and } \varepsilon' : \tau \;\vdash\; \varepsilon\varepsilon' : \tau'$$

$$\xi : \tau \Rightarrow \varepsilon : \tau' \;\vdash\; (\lambda\xi : \tau\,.\,\varepsilon : \tau') : \tau \to \tau'$$

An expression that does not satisfy the rules is not well typed. This is a conservative approach because some expressions that would evaluate correctly are rejected.

1 + if true then 2 else true

would always evaluate to 3 in the untyped λ-calculus but **Int** × **Bool** does not match the types of the branches of 'if' (Cond) and so the expression is not well typed. In programming language terms, the untyped λ-calculus has dynamic or run-time type checking. The typed λ-calculi have static type checking.

It is impossible to program self-applicative expressions such as **Y** in this system because recursive types cannot be constructed and Fortune, Leivant and O'Donnell [18] have shown that all well typed expressions have a normal form.

Attempting to give types to the components of **Y**,

Y = λG . (λg . G(gg)(λg . G(gg))
Y: (T → T) → T   for some T
G: T → T
g: U   where U = U → T

and the type U of g cannot be created in the simple system.

A λ-expression represents a function. A type represents a domain. **Int** represents the domain of integers, + represents disjoint union, → function domain and so on. The question of what a recursive type expression might represent is addressed later.

The *typed λ-calculus* is extended to allow recursive types.

τ ::= **Int** | **Bool** | . . . |	
τ × τ | τ + τ | τ → τ |	
'ξ |	type variable
μ'ξ . τ	fixed-point operator

μ is a fixed-point operator applicable to types, to enable recursive types to be written

g: μ'u. 'u → T   for some T

A variable 'ξ is bound by μ'ξ. Free type variables are not allowed in the typed λ-calculus.

As a shorthand, the definition of named types can be allowed and this example could then be written

g: U
where U = U → T   for some T

As has already been seen in §3.3.1 Algol-68 allows **modes** of this kind. Pascal allows some recursive types, but not **function** ones. ML allows recursive (abstract) types defined by the programmer.

3.4.1 *Type constructors*

Type constructors are considered next. An example is *list*:

type list('s) = {nil} + 's × list('s)

cons = λx: T, l: list(T). ⟨x, l⟩ for some T
null = λl: list(T). l = nil
hd = λl: list(T). if null(l) then wrong else l_1
tl = λl: list(T). if null(l) then wrong else l_2

The empty list is represented by nil. List is recursive. The example can be taken as an *implementation* of the list abstract data-type. This implementation would be hidden in an abstract data-type. For example, hd is applicable to any pair having the same structure as list, perhaps to stacks. Further, any function could dismantle the two components of a list – which would be dangerous if the implementation were changed. While these differences between abstract and implementation data-types are very important from the programming point of view, abstract types are not essential in the meta-language.

Many interesting and useful functions can be defined on lists:

length = λl: list(T). if null l then 0 else 1 + length(tl l)
map = λf: T → T′, l: list(T). if null l
then nil
else cons (f(hd l)) (map f (tl l)): list(T′)

As a shorthand, functions may be defined *by cases* or by pattern-matching when defined over a type such as list:

null nil = true
null ⟨a, b⟩ = false

length nil = 0
length ⟨a, b⟩ = 1 + length b

map f nil = nil
map f ⟨a, b⟩ = cons (f a) (map f b)

3.5 Polymorphic λ-calculus

The typed λ-calculus has the benefits of a statically typed programming language in allowing simple mechanical checking to detect many errors. However, some functions appear with the same 'code' but different types – a situation not unknown in Pascal and other languages – consider:

$$\mathrm{id}_{\mathrm{Int}} = \lambda x : \mathbf{Int}\,.\,x$$
$$\mathrm{id}_{\mathrm{Bool}} = \lambda x : \mathbf{Bool}\,.\,x$$

For any given type T, there is an identity function:

$$\mathrm{id}_{\mathrm{T}} = \lambda x : \mathrm{T}\,.\,x$$

This can be recognized by giving id the *polymorphic type*

$$\mathrm{id} : {'t} \to {'t}$$

where 't is a type variable. This is taken from ML [20, 37]. It can be read as, id has the type $\forall 't\ 't \to 't$. This type can be instantiated to **Int → Int, Bool → Bool** and even $('s \to 't) \to ('s \to 't)$. Free type variables are now allowed and are taken to be universally quantified.

Polymorphism very naturally allows *type inference*. Types may be omitted but an inference algorithm can correctly assign types to expressions and still detect type errors.

Examples

$k = \lambda x, y\,.\,x \quad k : {'s} \to {'t} \to {'s}$

$\mathrm{Cond} : {'s} \times {'s} \to \mathbf{Bool} \to {'s}$

$\circ : ({'t} \to {'u}) \times ({'s} \to {'t}) \to {'s} \to {'u}$

$_1 : {'s} \times {'t} \to {'s}$

$_2 : {'s} \times {'t} \to {'t}$

$\mathrm{nil} : \mathrm{list}({'s})$

$\mathrm{null} : \mathrm{list}({'s}) \to \mathbf{Bool}$

$\mathrm{hd} : \mathrm{list}({'s}) \to {'s}$

$\mathrm{tl} : \mathrm{list}({'s}) \to \mathrm{list}({'s})$

$\mathrm{cons} : {'s} \to \mathrm{list}({'s}) \to \mathrm{list}({'s})$

$\mathrm{twice} = \lambda f\,.\,f \circ f \quad \mathrm{twice} : ({'s} \to {'s}) \to {'s} \to {'s}$

Informally, the type of twice can be evaluated as follows.

$f : {'a}$ unknown

$\circ$ as above

${'a} = {'t} \to {'u} = {'s} \to {'t}$ so

${'s} = {'t} = {'u}$

${'a} = {'s} \to {'s}$ so

$\mathrm{twice} : ({'s} \to {'s}) \to {'s} \to {'s}$

The algorithm to do this is Robinson's unification algorithm [53] which will be met again in the chapter on Prolog, Ch 9.

The polymorphism and type inference described here are in the style of ML. The polymorphism is a subset of Reynold's second-order typed λ-calculus [51] where the identity function would have the type

$$\text{id}: \Lambda\text{'t}.\text{'t} \rightarrow \text{'t}$$

and Λ indicates *type abstraction*.

$$\text{id } \mathbf{Int} = (\Lambda\text{'t}.\text{'t} \rightarrow \text{'t})\mathbf{Int} = \mathbf{Int} \rightarrow \mathbf{Int}$$

$$\text{id } \mathbf{Bool} = (\Lambda\text{'t}.\text{'t} \rightarrow \text{'t})\mathbf{Bool} = \mathbf{Bool} \rightarrow \mathbf{Bool}$$

Type systems of this kind are still a field of research, witness the recent conference on the semantics of data-types [31] and papers in recent symposia on the principles of programming languages [1, 2].

3.6 Exercises

1. Evaluate

   k k 3
   k(k 3)
   If nasty = λf . f(f) evaluate

   nasty id
   nasty (k 3)
   nasty nasty

2. Given the list type, cons, hd, tl, null, if (or Cond) give a λ-expression for 'insert' where, for example,

   insert + 0 nil = 0
   insert + 0 ⟨1, 2, 3⟩ = 6
   insert op v nil = v
   insert op v $\langle l_1, l_2, \ldots\rangle = \text{v op}(l_1, \text{op}(l_2 \ldots))$
   What does the following function do?

   f = λx, l . insert or false (map (curry = x) l)

3. Give polymorphic types for curry and uncurry. Evaluate and give the types of

   uncurry curry
   uncurry uncurry

4. For the programming languages that you know (Ada, BCPL, C, Lisp, ...?) determine whether **Y** can be programmed in them.

4
Lattices

The assumption that data-types in a programming language might denote arbitrary sets leads to a contradiction. This means that expressions written in λ-notation, particularly recursive expressions, might be meaningless in the sense that there is nothing that they can be said to stand for. To correct matters, lattices are defined, and under reasonable conditions a recursive definition in λ-notation has at least one solution and, what is more, a special solution which it is natural to take as its meaning. The objective of this theory, developed by Scott, is to provide a *model* for the λ-notation – a collection of abstract objects that λ-expressions and types can be said to denote. Without these foundations, denotational definitions might be ambiguous or vacuous.

4.1 Cardinality

The *cardinality* of a finite set S, |S|, is the number of elements in S. $|\{1,2,3\}|=3$.

The *power set* of a set S, P(S), is the set of all subsets of S. $P(\{1,2,3\})=\{\{\,\},\{1\},\{2\},\{3\},\{1,2\},\{1,3\},\{2,3\},\{1,2,3\}\}$. Note, the empty set $\{\,\}$: P(S) and S: P(S) for any set S.

The set of all *mappings* of A into A, Map(A), is the set of all unrestricted partial or total functions from A into or onto A. $|Map(\{1,2,3\})|=64$.

Relations $=, \leqslant, <$ are defined on the cardinality of sets:

$|A|\leqslant|B|$ iff (if and only if) there is a total, 1-1 function from A into B

$|A|=|B|$ iff there is a total, 1-1 function from A onto B

$|A|<|B|$ iff $|A|\leqslant|B|$ and $|A|\neq|B|$

Although $=, \leqslant, <$ are chosen to look like the traditional equal, less than or equal, and less than, relations on real numbers, here they are defined on the cardinality even of infinite sets and it must be *shown* that they behave as expected!

Theorem (i) If $|A|\leqslant|B|$ and $|B|\leqslant|C|$ then $|A|\leqslant|C|$.

(ii) $|A|=|A|$.
(iii) (Schroeder–Bernstein) If $|A| \leqslant |B|$ and $|B| \leqslant |A|$ then $|A|=|B|$.

Proof (i) Given f: $A \to B$ and g: $B \to C$, where f and g total 1-1 and into, $g \circ f$: $A \to C$ is also total, 1-1 and into so $|A| \leqslant |C|$.

(ii) id: $A \to A$ shows $|A|=|A|$.

(iii) Given f: $A \to B$, g: $B \to A$, f and g total, 1-1, into. Define $g^{-1}(a)=\{b \mid g(b)=a\}$, then either $g^{-1}(a)=\{b\}$ for some b in B, or $g^{-1}(a)=\{\ \}$. That is, either a has a *parent* b in B or it has no parent.

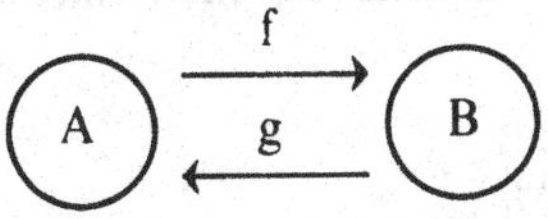

Define

$A_1=\{a \mid a$ has a parentless ancestor in $A\}$
$A_2=\{a \mid a$ has a parentless ancestor in $B\}$
$A_3=\{a \mid a$ has infinite ancestry$\}$

The three cases are exclusive and together make up A. $A=A_1 \cup A_2 \cup A_3$. Even if $g^{-1}(a)=\{\ \}$, a: A_1.

Similarly define f^{-1} and

$B_1=\{b \mid b$ has a parentless ancestor in $A\}$
$B_2=\{b \mid b$ has a parentless ancestor in $B\}$
$B_3=\{b \mid b$ has infinite ancestry$\}$

$B=B_1 \cup B_2 \cup B_3$.

f: $A_1 \to B_1$ is 1-1 onto
g: $B_2 \to A_2$ is 1-1 onto
f: $A_3 \to B_3$ is 1-1 onto

Now define h: $A \to B$

$$\begin{aligned} h(a) &= f(a) && \text{if a in } A_1 \cup A_3 \\ &= g^{-1}(a) && \text{if a in } A_2 \end{aligned}$$

It is easy to check that h is 1-1, onto, so $|A|=|B|$. □

Technically, these results mean that $\leqslant$ is an order and that $=, \leqslant, <$ really do behave as expected even on infinite cardinalities. Next, Cantor's result shows that a set is definitely smaller than its power set; this is one of the classics of set theory.

Theorem (Cantor)
$|A| < |P(A)|$.

Proof $a \to \{a\}$ is a total, 1-1, function of A into P(A) so $|A| \leqslant |P(A)|$.
Suppose $|A| = |P(A)|$, i.e. $\exists f: A \to P(A)$ which is 1-1 and onto. Define

$$B = \{a: A \mid \sim a: f(a)\}$$

then B is a subset of A, $B \subseteq A$, B: P(A). So there must be an a_0 such that $f(a_0) = B$. But now if a_0 is in B then a_0 is not in B and vice versa. This is a contradiction, so f cannot exist, so $|A| < |P(A)|$. □

The technique used in the last proof is called diagonalization. Finally, if A has at least two elements, the mappings of A, Map(A), are at least as numerous as the elements of P(A) – so there are more of them than elements of A too.

Theorem If $|A| > 1$ then $|P(A)| \leqslant |Map(A)|$.

Proof Choose a_0: A and a_1: A, $a_0 \neq a_1$. Given B: P(A), $B \subseteq A$, let

$$\begin{aligned} b(a) &= a_0 \quad \text{if } a: B \\ &= a_1 \quad \text{otherwise} \end{aligned}$$

Mapping B onto b gives a total, 1-1 function from P(A) into Map(A). □

Corollary $|A| < |P(A)| \leqslant |Map(A)|$

This is very awkward because many programming languages allow the manipulation of some domain, **Value**, where **Value** includes some basic domains such as **Int**, **Bool**, **Char** and unions, multiples and functions over these values:

$$\mathbf{Value} = \mathbf{Bv} + (\mathbf{Value} + \mathbf{Value}) + (\mathbf{Value} \times \mathbf{Value}) + (\mathbf{Value} \to \mathbf{Value})$$

where

$$\mathbf{Bv} = \mathbf{Int} + \mathbf{Bool} + \mathbf{Char} + \ldots$$

But if **Value → Value** is equal to Map(**Value**) this is impossible on grounds of cardinality. The only way out of the dilemma is to restrict the number of mappings in **Value → Value** a great deal.

The equality above is also impossible on a technicality. The right-hand side is a disjoint sum and, expanding it out,

$$\begin{aligned} \mathbf{Value} = \mathbf{Bv} &+ ((\mathbf{Bv} + \ldots) + (\mathbf{Bv} + \ldots)) + (\ldots \times \ldots) \\ &+ (\mathbf{Bv} + (\mathbf{Value} + \mathbf{Value}) + \ldots + \mathbf{Value} \to \mathbf{Value}) \\ &\to (\mathbf{Bv} + (\mathbf{Value} + \mathbf{Value}) + \ldots + \mathbf{Value} \to \mathbf{Value}) \end{aligned}$$

The right-hand side does not include functions on **Bv** directly; however, reading the = as 'is isomorphic to' removes the technicality but not the cardinality argument. $f: A \to B$ can be identified with $f': A + B \to A + B$ where $f'\langle a, 1\rangle = \langle f(a), 2\rangle$ and so on.

4.1.1 *Halting problem*

The best-known example of an element of Map(**Value**) that is not computable, in other words, not in **Value** → **Value**, is the halting problem. There is no procedure which will determine if an arbitrary procedure will halt when applied to some arbitrary data. If there were, the following procedure could be written:

```
procedure paradox(p)
  function halts(q; d): boolean;
    ... assume written ...
begin {paradox}
  while halts(p, p) do {loop}
end
```

Now ask if paradox(paradox) terminates. It is halts, halts(paradox, paradox) returns true so it loops. If it loops then halts(paradox, paradox) returns false so it halts. This is a contradiction so halts cannot be written.

An English description of paradox is: paradox is a procedure which loops when applied to those procedures which do not loop when applied to themselves. Substituting barber for paradox, man for procedure, and shaves for loops-when-applied-to, gives a description of a well-known individual.

4.2 Lattice structure

The formulation of lattices used here is to add a special least or undefined element, $\perp$ or bottom, to all elementary domains and to define a partial order or approximation $\sqsubseteq$. This allows all functions to be total. $\sqsubseteq$ then induces a similar structure on compound domains $A \times B$ and $A + B$. With some plausible restrictions, $A \to B$ has the same structure and then all functions $f: S \to S$ have a fixed point. What is called a lattice here, many other authors would call a complete partial order (CPO)†, but lattice is shorter.

There are alternatives, and Scott [55] and Stoy [58] also add a most defined or 'over-defined' element, $\top$ or top. However, top does not have an entirely satisfactory intuitive role and is not necessary so it is not adopted here.

4.2.1 *Partial orders*

A *partial order* on a set S is a relation on S that is

transitive: if $x \sqsubseteq y$ and $y \sqsubseteq z$ then $x \sqsubseteq z$

† Also a contradiction in terms!

antisymmetric: if $x \sqsubseteq y$ and $y \sqsubseteq x$ then $x = y$
reflexive: for all x in S, $x \sqsubseteq x$

A partial order is a very common sort of relation.

Example

$\subseteq$ on P({1, 2, 3}) is a partial order.
if $x \subseteq y$ and $y \subseteq z$ then $x \subseteq z$
if $x \subseteq y$ and $y \subseteq x$ then $x = y$
for all t in P({1, 2, 3}), $t \subseteq t$.

Note that some pairs of elements, such as {1,2} and {2,3}, are *incomparable* under $\subseteq$, they overlap but neither one is contained in the other.

A *lower bound* of a subset A of set S with a partial order is an element z in S such that, for all x in A, $z \sqsubseteq x$. Lower bounds may not exist for arbitrary A, S, $\sqsubseteq$.

Example { } is the only lower bound for all of P({1, 2, 3}). { } and {1} are lower bounds for {{1,2}, {1,3}}.

An *upper bound* of a subset A of S is an element z in S such that, for all x in A, $x \sqsubseteq z$. Again, upper bounds may not exist.

Example {1, 2, 3} is the only upper bound of {{1,2}, {1,3}}. {1,2} and {1, 2, 3} are upper bounds for {{1,2}}.

A *least upper bound* (LUB) of a subset A of S, written $\sqcup A$, is an upper bound of A, such that, for any upper bound x of A, $\sqcup A \sqsubseteq x$.

Example {1, 2, 3} is an upper bound of {{1},{2}} but {1, 2} is the least upper bound.

An *ascending chain* is a sequence of elements of S such that

$$x_1 \sqsubseteq x_2 \sqsubseteq x_3 \sqsubseteq \ldots$$

An upper bound or a least upper bound of a chain is an upper bound or a least upper bound of the set of elements in the chain.

A *complete lattice* S, $\sqsubseteq$ is a set S with a partial order $\sqsubseteq$, such that there is an element $\perp$ for which $\perp \sqsubseteq x$ for all x in L, and in which every ascending chain $x_1 \sqsubseteq x_2 \sqsubseteq x_3 \ldots$ has a least upper bound.

Example P({1, 2, 3}), $\subseteq$ is a complete lattice.

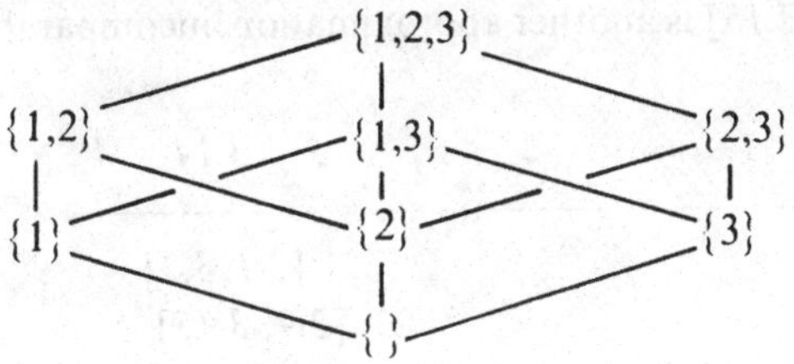

A complete lattice may be drawn, as above, with a line from x up to y if $x \sqsubseteq y$.

Loosely speaking, any lattice with a finite number of levels and a pointed '$\bot$' is complete. Not all lattices with an infinite number of levels are complete.

The elementary domains can at last be defined as complete lattices with a partial order, $\sqsubseteq$ or *approximation*, and the following structure:

Bool:

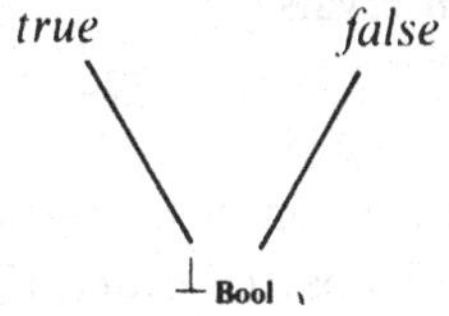

Int:

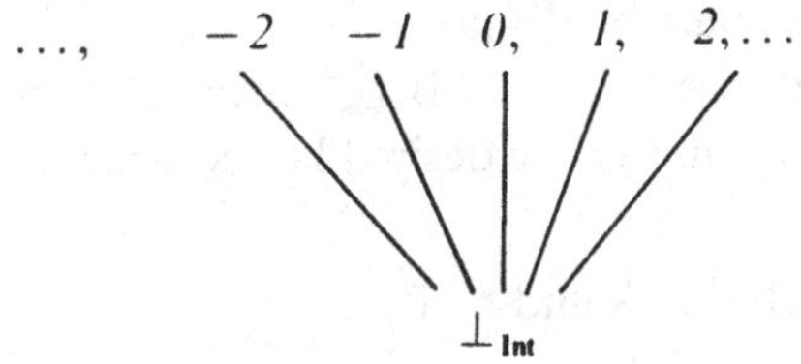

These are called flat lattices because the only addition consists of an undefined element $\bot$. The *least* element, $\bot_D$, of each domain D can be thought of as a completely undefined or unspecified element. It is analogous to the undefined variable in a program. Note that $\bot_{Int}$, $\bot_{Bool}$ and so on are quite distinct, but are often written undecorated as $\bot$ with the domain deduced from context.

Example Intervals on the real line form a complete-lattice under inclusion. Let $[x, y] = \{z \mid x \leqslant z \leqslant y\}$, define $[a, b] \sqsubseteq [c, d]$ iff $[a, b] \subseteq [c, d]$. An interval $[x, y]$ can be thought of as an approximation to the real numbers it contains. The worst or least approximation of all is $[-\infty, +\infty]$. $[3, 4]$ is a rather poor approximation to π. $[3.1, 3.2]$ is a rather better one. [*2.9, 3.15*] is another approximation, incomparable with [*3, 4*].

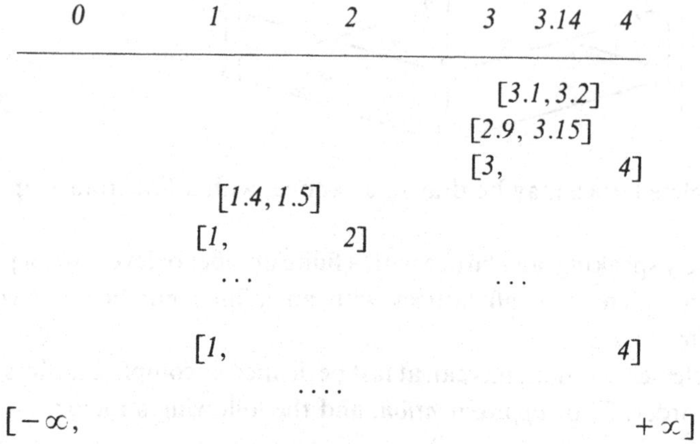

Real-Intervals

4.2.2 ***Lattice operations***

Product, union and disjoint union were previously defined for domains before the introduction of the partial order, $\sqsubseteq$. The definitions were valid as far as they went, but now the resulting partial order on such constructed domains must be defined.

Given complete lattices A, $\sqsubseteq'$ and B, $\sqsubseteq''$, there are two ways of defining their *direct product*. Both give the desired lattice structure. The non-strict direct product is:

$$A \times B = \{\langle a, b\rangle \mid a\colon A \text{ and } b\colon B\}$$

and

$$\langle a,b\rangle \sqsubseteq \langle c,d\rangle \text{ iff } a \sqsubseteq' c \text{ and } b \sqsubseteq'' d$$

The strict direct product is formed by identifying

$$\forall a\colon A,\ b\colon B\ \langle a, \bot_B\rangle = \langle \bot_A, b\rangle = \bot_{A\times B}$$

An element of the strict product cannot be 'half' defined.

Note that these define new partial orders on the set of elements A × B. It is not hard to see that both make A × B a complete lattice. Any chain $\langle a_1, b_1\rangle \sqsubseteq \langle a_2, b_2\rangle \sqsubseteq \ldots$ gives a chain $a_1 \sqsubseteq' a_2 \sqsubseteq' \ldots$ in A, and a chain $b_1 \sqsubseteq'' b_2 \sqsubseteq'' \ldots$ in B. $\langle \sqcup\{a_i\}, \sqcup\{b_j\}\rangle$ is a least upper bound for the original ascending chain.

Given complete lattices A, $\sqsubseteq'$ and B, $\sqsubseteq''$ there are two ways of defining their sum. The *coalesced disjoint sum* is:

$$A + B = \{\langle a, 1\rangle \mid a\colon A\} \cup \{\langle b, 2\rangle \mid b\colon B\}$$

but

$$\langle \bot_A, 1\rangle = \langle \bot_B, 2\rangle = \bot_{A+B}$$
$$\langle a, 1\rangle \sqsubseteq \langle a', 1\rangle \text{ iff } a \sqsubseteq' a'$$

and

$$\langle b,2\rangle \sqsubseteq \langle b',2\rangle \text{ iff } b \sqsubseteq'' b'$$
$$\langle a, 1\rangle \text{ and } \langle b, 2\rangle \text{ are otherwise incomparable}$$

The *separated disjoint sum* is:

$$A+B=\{\langle a, 1\rangle \mid a\colon A\} \cup \{\langle b, 2\rangle \mid b\colon B\} \cup \{\bot_{A+B}\}$$

where

$$\bot_{A+B} \sqsubseteq \langle \bot_A, 1\rangle$$

and

$$\bot_{A+B} \sqsubseteq \langle \bot_B, 2\rangle$$

otherwise $\sqsubseteq$ is as before. In the separated sum, $\langle \bot_A, 1\rangle$ is equivalent to an element of A, although undefined, and is quite distinct from $\bot_{A+B}$ and $\langle \bot_B, 2\rangle$.

It is easy to see that, coalesced or separated, A + B is a complete lattice. $\sqsubseteq$ is a partial order. An ascending chain $x_1 \sqsubseteq x_2 \sqsubseteq \ldots$ in A + B may repeat $\bot_{A+B}$ forever or eventually climb into either $A \times \{1\}$ or $B \times \{2\}$. In any case $\bot_{A+B}$ or the least upper bound in A or B makes a least upper bound for the original chain.

In a statically typed language, the factorial of a negative number can be said to be the undefined **Int**, fact$(-3) = \bot_{\text{Int}}$, and it would be appropriate for **Value** to be the separated sum of **Int** and some other domains in its semantics. In a language with dynamic types this distinction may not be useful and the coalesced sum might be used.

Example

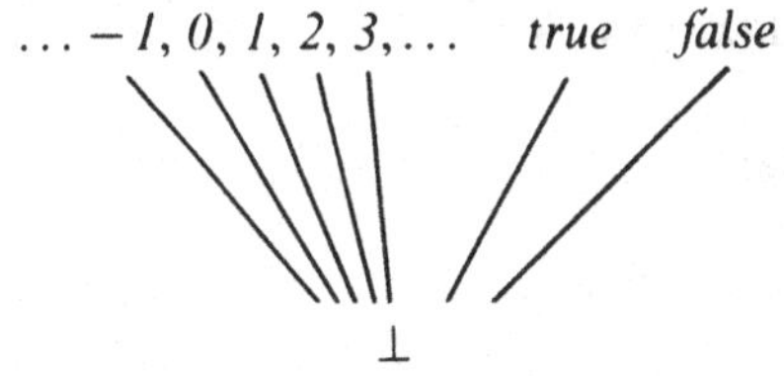

Coalesced **Int** + **Bool**

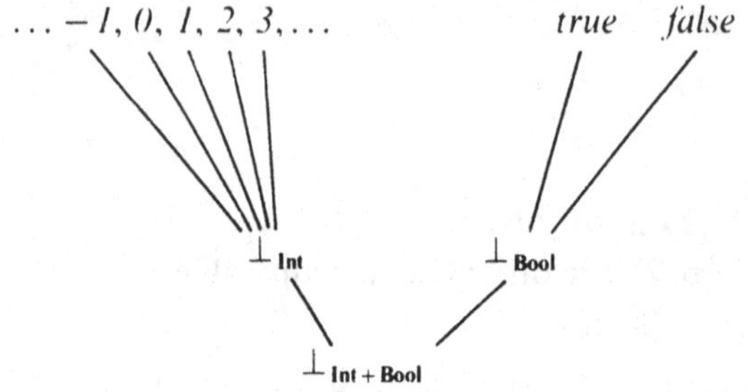

Separated **Int + Bool**

The non-strict product and the separated sum are used by default. Frequently it does not matter which choice is made in the sense that consistent semantics can be based on more than one choice.

4.2.3 *Lattice of functions*

The functions on a complete lattice S, ⊑ are examined next. A partial order is defined on S → S. Restricting membership of S → S in certain plausible ways makes S → S a complete lattice and all functions in S → S have a fixed point which means that all (recursive) equations have a solution or meaning. In fact they each have a least fixed point or least specified solution and this is taken to be the natural meaning.

If S, ⊑ is a complete lattice, define ⊑′ on Map(S) and therefore on S → S by

f⊑′g iff f(x)⊑g(x) ∀x: S

then ⊑′ is a partial order on S → S:

transitive:

if f⊑′g and g⊑′h then
f(x)⊑g(x) and g(x)⊑h(x) ∀x: S
so f(x)⊑h(x) ∀x: s
as ⊑ is a partial order
so f⊑′h

antisymmetric:

f⊑′g and g⊑′f implies
f(x)⊑g(x) and g(x)⊑f(x) ∀x: S
so f(x) = g(x) ∀x: S
so f = g

reflexive:

f(x)⊑f(x) ∀x: S
so f⊑′f

The set of all mappings of S to S, Map(S), $\sqsubseteq'$, forms a complete lattice although as we saw before in §4.1 it is too large to be the computable functions. Let $\bot' = \lambda x.\bot$: Map(S) then $\bot' \sqsubseteq' f$ for all f in Map(S). If $f_1 \sqsubseteq' f_2 \sqsubseteq' f_3 \ldots$ is a chain in Map(S) then for any x in S $f_1(x) \sqsubseteq f_2(x) \sqsubseteq \ldots$ is a chain in S so it has a least upper bound X; let $(\sqcup\{f_i\})(x) = X$. It can be seen that $\sqcup\{f_i\}$ really is a least upper bound for $\{f_i\}$, so Map(S), $\sqsubseteq'$ is complete.

A *monotonic* function f on a lattice S, $\sqsubseteq$ is one for which $x \sqsubseteq y$ implies $f(x) \sqsubseteq f(y)$. Intuitively one cannot get more information out of f unless more information is put in. This is enshrined as garbage-in-garbage-out (GIGO) in the folklore.

A *continuous* function f on a complete lattice S, $\sqsubseteq$ is one that preserves least upper bounds. That is, if $A = a_1 \sqsubseteq a_2 \sqsubseteq a_3 \ldots$ is an ascending chain then $f(\sqcup A) = \sqcup(f(A))$ where $f(A) = \{f(a) \mid a: A\}$.

Continuity does not have quite such an obvious interpretation as monotonicity. A program or algorithm is a finite description of a function. Unfolding a recursive program more and more times gives better and better approximations to the function. Given

$$F = \lambda f.\lambda x.\text{if } x = 0 \text{ then } 1 \text{ else } x \times f(x-1)$$

the idea is that if there is a chain of functions $f_1 \sqsubseteq' f_2 \sqsubseteq' f_3 \ldots$ which are better and better approximations to a limit function $\sqcup\{f_i\}$ then $F(\sqcup\{f_i\}) = \sqcup\{F(f_i)\}$. That is, there are no surprises at the limit; it is possible to predict the behaviour of F on $\sqcup\{f_i\}$ from its behaviour on each f_i.

Finally, if S, $\sqsubseteq$ is a complete lattice, define $S \to S$ to be the set of total, monotonic, continuous functions from S to S with the induced partial order $\sqsubseteq'$!

Theorem $S \to S$ is a complete lattice.

Proof We know $\sqsubseteq'$ is a partial order. $\lambda x.\bot: S \to S$ is monotonic and continuous and the least element of $S \to S$. It is only necessary to show that if

$$f_1 \sqsubseteq' f_2 \sqsubseteq' f_3 \ldots$$

is an ascending chain and $ff = \sqcup\{f_i\}$, then ff is monotonic and continuous.

(i) If $x \sqsubseteq y$ in S then $f_i(x) \sqsubseteq f_i(y)$ for all i because the f_is are monotonic. So $ff(x) = \sqcup\{f_i(x)\} \sqsubseteq \sqcup\{f_i(y)\} = ff(y)$.

(ii) Suppose there is an ascending chain in S

$$x_1 \sqsubseteq x_2 \sqsubseteq x_3 \ldots$$

we want to show that $\sqcup\{ff\{x_i\}\} = ff(\sqcup\{x_i\})$.

$$ff(\sqcup\{x_j\}) = \sqcup_i\{f_i(\sqcup_j\{x_j\})\}$$
$$= \sqcup_i\{\sqcup_j\{f_i\{x_j\}\}\} \text{ as each } f_i \text{ is continuous}$$

we want this to equal

$$\sqcup_j\{\sqcup_i\{f_i\{x_j\}\}\} = \sqcup\{ff\{x_j\}\}$$

The central step, interchanging the order of the two $\sqcup$s, is not obvious.

$$
\begin{array}{c|ccccc}
\sqcup\{x_j\} & f_1(\sqcup\{x_j\}) & f_2(\sqcup\{x_j\}) & f_3(\sqcup\{x_j\}) & & ??? \\
\cdots & & & & & \\
\sqsubseteq & & & & & \\
x_3 & f_1(x_3) & f_2(x_3) & f_3(x_3) & \ldots & ff(x_3) \\
\sqsubseteq & & & & & \\
x_2 & f_1(x_2) & f_2(x_2) & f_3(x_2) & \ldots & ff(x_2) \\
\sqsubseteq & & & & & \\
x_1 & f_1(x_1) & f_2(x_1) & f_3(x_1) & \ldots & ff(x_1) \\
\hline
 & f_1 \sqsubseteq & f_2 \sqsubseteq & f_3 \sqsubseteq & \ldots & ff = \sqcup\{f_i\}
\end{array}
$$

If the step is valid, the limit of the top row is equal to the limit of the right-hand column above. Note that each row above is ascending going from left to right as is each column going upwards.

$$\text{for all } k, j \quad f_k(x_j) \sqsubseteq \sqcup_i\{f_i(x_j)\}$$

so

$$\sqcup_j\{f_i\{x_j\}\} \sqsubseteq \sqcup_j\{\sqcup_i\{f_i\{x_j\}\}\}$$

so

$$\sqcup_i\{\sqcup_j\{f_i\{x_j\}\}\} \sqsubseteq \sqcup_j\{\sqcup_i\{f_i\{x_j\}\}\}$$

In addition,

$$\text{for all } k, j \quad f_k(x_j) \sqsubseteq \sqcup_j\{f_k\{x_j\}\}$$
$$\sqcup_i\{f_i(x_j)\} \sqsubseteq \sqcup_i\{\sqcup_j\{f_i\{x_j\}\}\}$$
$$\sqcup_j\{\sqcup_i\{f_i\{x_j\}\}\} \sqsubseteq \sqcup_i\{\sqcup_j\{f_i\{x_j\}\}\}$$

so finally

$$\sqcup_i\{\sqcup_j\{f_i\{x_j\}\}\} = \sqcup_j\{\sqcup_i\{f_i\{x_j\}\}\} \quad \square$$

So the elementary domains are turned into complete lattices and derived domains $A \times B$, $A + B$ and $A \rightarrow B$ are also complete lattices.

Example

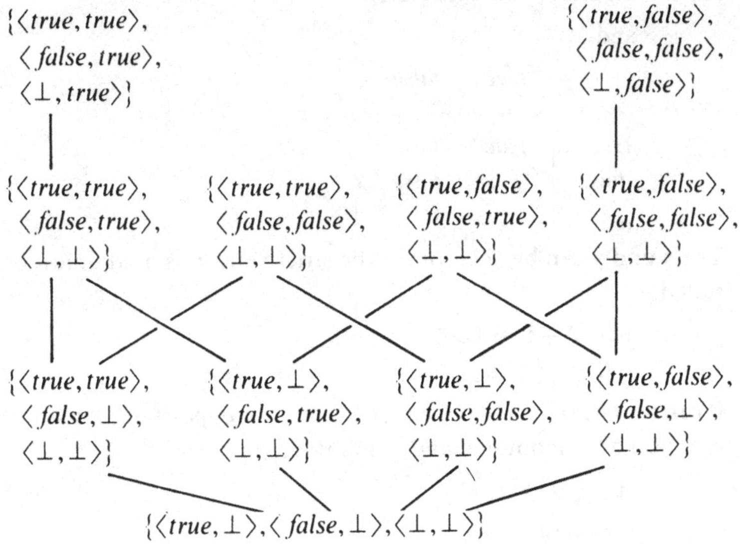

Bool→Bool

Note that certain mappings such as {⟨*true*, ⊥⟩, ⟨*false*, *true*⟩, ⟨⊥, *true*⟩} are not allowed in **Bool → Bool** because they are not monotonic.

4.2.4 ***Basic functions***

The basic functions used already are, or can be made, monotonic and continuous.

x	not x
true	*false*
false	*true*
⊥	⊥

or

	true	*false*	⊥
true	*true*	*true*	x
false	*true*	*false*	⊥
⊥	y	⊥	⊥

The x and y can each be *true* or $\perp$, the strict 'or' in which $x=y=\perp$ is preferred unless otherwise stated.

and

	true	*false*	$\perp$
true	*true*	*false*	$\perp$
false	*false*	*false*	x
$\perp$	$\perp$	y	$\perp$

The x and y can be *false* or $\perp$; the strict version is used unless otherwise stated.

isA: A + B → **Bool**

isA $\perp_{A+B} = \perp_{Bool}$

It can also be shown that Cond, projection, composition, construction and injection are monotonic and continuous.

$\perp_{A\times B}[1] = \perp_A$

$\perp_{A\times B}[2] = \perp_B$

Cond is strict on the control value:

$\text{Cond}\langle p, q\rangle \perp_{Bool} = \perp_{S\to S}$

It is also strict on its first argument which is another reason to note the definition of the **if** command in §2.4 for, although one branch of an **if** may yield an undefined state in certain circumstances, the **if** is only undefined if *both* branches are always undefined, equal to $\perp_{(S\to S)\times(S\to S)}$.

4.2.5 Least fixed points

Theorem If S, $\sqsubseteq$ is a complete lattice and f: S → S (so f is monotonic and continuous) then f has a fixed point.

Proof $\perp \sqsubseteq f(\perp)$ because S is complete. $f(\perp) \sqsubseteq f(f(\perp))$ because f is monotonic. So

$$\perp \sqsubseteq f(\perp) \sqsubseteq f(f(\perp)) \ldots$$

is an ascending chain, so it has a least upper bound u.

$$\begin{aligned} f(u) &= f(\sqcup\{f^i(\perp)\}) \\ &= \sqcup\{f\{f^i(\perp)\}\} \\ &= \sqcup\{f^i(\perp)\} \\ &= u \end{aligned}$$

So u is a fixed point of f. u is the *least fixed point*, for, if v were another, $\perp \sqsubseteq v$ so $f(\perp) \sqsubseteq f(v) = v$ and $f^i(\perp) \sqsubseteq v$ by induction. So $u \sqsubseteq v$. □

This result may be rather surprising in the face of functions such as

$$\text{succ} = \lambda x \,.\, x + 1$$

but succ has a fixed point too, $\bot_{\text{Int}}$.

Example

Given any set S, $\langle P(S), \subseteq\rangle$ is a complete lattice. { } is the least element. $\sqcup\{S_1 \subseteq S_2 \subseteq S_3 \ldots\} = \bigcup_{i>0} S_i$.

Let $S = \{(,)\}^*$. Define f: $P(S) \rightarrow P(S)$ by

$$f(B) = B \cup \{(x) \mid x{:}\ B\} \cup \{xy \mid x, y{:}\ B\} \cup \{(\,)\}$$

It can be shown that f is monotonic and continuous. Therefore f has a least fixed point, L, and it is the language of matched brackets, usually given by the BNF:

$$s ::= (s) \mid s\ s \mid (\,)$$

The least fixed point of f is the smallest set containing { } and closed under f, or fixed by it.

Example Recall F:

$$F = \lambda f \,.\, \lambda x \,.\, \text{if } x = 0 \text{ then } 1 \text{ else } x \times f(x-1)$$

The completely undefined function is

$$\begin{aligned}\bot' &= (\lambda x \,.\, \bot){:}\ \mathbf{Int} \rightarrow \mathbf{Int}\\ &= \{\ldots, \langle -1, \bot\rangle, \langle 0, \bot\rangle, \langle 1, \bot\rangle, \ldots\}\end{aligned}$$

Apply F to $\bot'$:

$$\begin{aligned}&F\ \bot'\\ &= \lambda x \,.\, \text{if } x = 0 \text{ then } 1 \text{ else } x \times \bot'(x-1)\\ &= \lambda x \,.\, \text{if } x = 0 \text{ then } 1 \text{ else } \bot\\ &= \{\ldots, \langle -1, \bot\rangle, \langle 0, 1\rangle, \langle 1, \bot\rangle, \ldots\}.\end{aligned}$$

This is a very slightly more defined function.

$$\begin{aligned}&F(F\ \bot')\\ &= \lambda x \,.\, \text{if } x = 0 \text{ then } 1 \text{ else } x \times (F\ \bot')(x-1)\\ &= \lambda x \,.\, \text{if } x = 0 \text{ then } 1 \text{ else } x \times (\text{if } x - 1 = 0 \text{ then } 1 \text{ else } (x-1) * \bot'(x-2))\\ &= \lambda x \,.\, \text{if } x = 0 \text{ then } 1 \text{ else if } x = 1 \text{ then } 1 \text{ else } \bot\\ &= \{\ldots, \langle -1, \bot\rangle, \langle 0, 1\rangle, \langle 1, 1\rangle, \langle 2, \bot\rangle, \ldots\}.\end{aligned}$$

This is yet more defined. The picture should now be clear; $F^n(\bot')$ is defined, and agrees with the real factorial function, on the integers $\{0 \mathinner{..} n-1\}$, elsewhere it is undefined. As n gets bigger, the function is a better and better approximation to factorial. Factorial is the least fixed point of F. This is taken to be the meaning of the recursive definition

$$\text{fact} = \lambda x\,.\,\text{if } x = 0 \text{ then } 1 \text{ else } x \times \text{fact}(x-1)$$

The least fixed point is chosen, as opposed to some other one, because it embodies exactly the information that can be deduced from the definition and the information that *must* be deduced from it.

4.3 Recursive domains

Some recursive types have already been used on the tacit assumption that the recursive domains they denote exist. In the definition of the fixed-point operator **Y** (§ 3.3.1) there was a type U = U → T and it was noted (§ 4.1) that some programming languages include as data-types

$$\mathbf{Value} = \mathbf{Bv} + (\mathbf{Value} + \mathbf{Value}) + (\mathbf{Value} \times \mathbf{Value}) + (\mathbf{Value} \to \mathbf{Value})$$

4.3.1 *Lists and sequences*

Type constructors such as 'list' were previously used. These can be recursive:

$$\text{type list('t)} = \{\text{nil}\} + \text{'t} \times \text{list('t)}$$

There are two meanings for list as the product is strict or non-strict. If the product is strict, list(T) can be taken to represent T*, the lattice of finite sequences over T. If the product is not strict, list(T) must contain the ascending chain

$$\bot \sqsubseteq \langle t, \bot \rangle \sqsubseteq \langle t, t, \bot \rangle \sqsubseteq \ldots$$
$$\text{where } \bot, t : T$$

For list(T) to be complete, the limit of the chain must be in list(T)

$$\langle t, t, \ldots \rangle = \prod_{i>0} t : \text{list(T)}$$

This is the infinite list of 't' repeated; it can be represented by the cyclic data structure

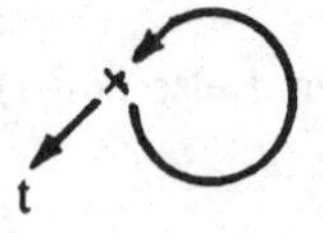

and this is certainly computable. In this case list(T) must contain other infinite lists.

Example

```
filterout p (cons a b)=if not(p a)
                         then cons a (filterout p b)
                         else filterout p b
from n=cons n (from (n+1))
multipleof n m=m mod n=0
sieve (cons a b)=cons a (sieve (filterout (multipleof a) b))
primes=sieve(from 2)
```

If evaluated in normal order or by *lazy evaluation*, primes is the infinite list of all prime numbers. Some interpreters for some functional languages [22, 23, 64] use normal order and the example is typical of many interesting programming techniques.

Even in a programming language without lazy evaluation, it may be possible to program the same effect explicitly with functions; see for example Burge [6].

```
stream('t)={ } → 't × stream('t)
hds s: stream('t)=s( )₁
tls s: stream('t)=s( )₂
scons a: 't s: stream('t) ( )=⟨a, s⟩
from n ( )=scons n (from(n+1))
```

The primes example can be rewritten using stream, hds, tls, scons instead of list, hd, tl, cons.

Briefly, a model for the domain equation

$$\mathbf{Value} = \mathbf{Bv} + (\mathbf{Value} \times \mathbf{Value}) + (\mathbf{Value} \to \mathbf{Value}) + \ldots$$

with the strict product, includes a model for the equation with the non-strict product. In the next section the recursive function domain is constructed explicitly.

The non-strict product is adopted by default unless otherwise stated. In modelling Pascal **records**, say, the strict product may be more natural – as Pascal does not use lazy evaluation – but valid records can be identified with a subset of the non-strict product in any case.

4.3.2 *Inverse-limit construction*

Scott [55] gave the first construction for a domain $\mathbf{D} \equiv \mathbf{D} \to \mathbf{D}$. This provides a *model* for the untyped λ-calculus. Wadsworth [66] examined this and other models, including models for the λ-calculus with atoms (constants), $\mathbf{E} \equiv \mathbf{A} + (\mathbf{E} \to \mathbf{E})$. How this method, known as the *inverse-limit construction*, builds a lattice which is a solution to

$$\mathbf{Value} \equiv \mathbf{Bv} + (\mathbf{Value} \rightarrow \mathbf{Value})$$

is sketched below. Later Scott [56] gave another model based on the power set of the integers. The λ-expression for **Y**, § 3.3.1, is a *syntactic* definition. Scott's models construct *abstract* objects that such expressions can be taken to denote. This means the expressions really do stand for something and are not vacuous.

The inverse-limit construction begins with a sequence of domains:

$$\mathbf{V}_0 = \mathbf{Bv}$$
$$\mathbf{V}_1 = \mathbf{Bv} + (\mathbf{V}_0 \rightarrow \mathbf{V}_0)$$
$$\ldots$$
$$\mathbf{V}_i = \mathbf{Bv} + (\mathbf{V}_{i-1} \rightarrow \mathbf{V}_{i-1})$$
$$\ldots$$

What is required is the limit domain of this sequence, or something like it. It might be tempting to take the sum of the $\mathbf{V}_i$ but this would *not* do, for it would only correspond to types containing a finite number of $\rightarrow$s and would not include μ't.'t $\rightarrow$ **Bv** for example. Instead a domain $\mathbf{V}_\infty$ is constructed to satisfy $\mathbf{V}_\infty = \mathbf{Bv} + (\mathbf{V}_\infty \rightarrow \mathbf{V}_\infty)$ in such a way that v: $\mathbf{V}_\infty$ can be taken to be a member of **Bv** or of $\mathbf{V}_\infty \rightarrow \mathbf{V}_\infty$ as appropriate. The idea is to use infinite sequences of $v_i : \mathbf{V}_i$.

An element of $\mathbf{V}_0 = \mathbf{Bv}$ can be treated as a member of $\mathbf{V}_1$, under the injection

$$in_0 x = \langle x, 1 \rangle : \mathbf{V}_1$$

$\mathbf{V}_1$ can be projected onto $\mathbf{V}_0$:

$$p_0 \langle x, 1 \rangle = x : \mathbf{V}_0$$
$$p_0 \langle f, 2 \rangle = \bot : \mathbf{V}_0$$

$$\mathbf{V}_0 \underset{p_0}{\overset{in_0}{\rightleftarrows}} \mathbf{V}_1$$

Note that

$$p_0 \circ in_0 = id : \mathbf{V}_0 \rightarrow \mathbf{V}_0 \text{ and}$$
$$in_0 \circ p_0 \sqsubseteq id : \mathbf{V}_1 \rightarrow \mathbf{V}_1$$

Going from $\mathbf{V}_0$ up to $\mathbf{V}_1$ and back, no information is lost. Going from $\mathbf{V}_1$ down to $\mathbf{V}_0$ and back, information may be lost but the result approximates or is consistent with the starting point.

Also required are injections and projections further up the chain

$$in_i : \mathbf{V}_i \rightarrow \mathbf{V}_{i+1}$$
$$p_i : \mathbf{V}_{i+1} \rightarrow \mathbf{V}_i$$

which preserve application, that is, if

$$v_{i+1}: \mathbf{V}_i \to \mathbf{V}_i \subseteq \mathbf{V}_{i+1}$$
$$v_i: \mathbf{V}_i$$

then

$$in_i(\; v_{i+1} v_i \;) = (in_{i+1} v_{i+1})(in_i v_i)$$

This is because it is necessary to treat $v_i: \mathbf{V}_i$ as an element of $\mathbf{V}_{i+1}$ later, and injecting the result of applying a function to a value should be the same as applying the injected function to the injected value. in_i and p_i must also satisfy

$$p_i \circ in_i = id: \mathbf{V}_i \to \mathbf{V}_i$$

and

$$in_i \circ p_i \sqsubseteq id: \mathbf{V}_{i+1} \to \mathbf{V}_{i+1}$$

as before, so that information is preserved in going up and down, and consistency is preserved in going down and then up.

$$\mathbf{V}_0 \underset{p_0}{\overset{in_0}{\rightleftarrows}} \mathbf{V}_1 \underset{p_1}{\overset{in_1}{\rightleftarrows}} \mathbf{V}_2 \underset{p_2}{\overset{in_2}{\rightleftarrows}} \mathbf{V}_3 \quad \ldots$$

This can be arranged if

$$in_{i+1} v_{i+1} = v_{i+1} \quad \text{if isBv } v_{i+1}$$

$$in_{i+1} v_{i+1} = in_i \circ v_{i+1} \circ p_i \quad \text{otherwise}$$

$$p_{i+1} v_{i+2} = v_{i+2} \quad \text{if isBv } v_{i+2}$$

$$p_{i+1} v_{i+2} = p_i \circ v_{i+2} \circ in_i \quad \text{otherwise}$$

With compositions of these functions, it is possible to consider $v_i: \mathbf{V}_i$ to be a member of any $\mathbf{V}_j$.

Define

$$\mathbf{V}_\infty = \{\langle v_i \rangle \mid v_i: \mathbf{V}_i,\; p_i v_{i+1} = v_i \;\forall i \geqslant 0\}$$
$$\subseteq \prod_{i \geqslant 0} \mathbf{V}_i$$

$\mathbf{V}_\infty$ consists of certain infinite tuples of elements of the $\mathbf{V}_i$.

It is possible to inject $v_i:\mathbf{V}_i$ into $\mathbf{V}_\infty$ by projecting v_i onto those $\mathbf{V}_j$ $j<i$ and injecting it into those $\mathbf{V}_k$ $k>i$ and constructing the corresponding tuple.

$$in_{i,\infty}: \mathbf{V}_i \to \mathbf{V}_\infty$$
$$p_{\infty,i}\langle v_0, \ldots v_i, \ldots \rangle = v_i: \mathbf{V}_\infty \to \mathbf{V}_i$$

It is convenient to *identify* v_i and $in_{i,\infty}(v_i)$ and consider them to be identical.

Example

$s = \lambda x: \mathbf{V}_0 . 7$

$\equiv \langle \bot, \lambda x: \mathbf{V}_0 . 7: \mathbf{V}_0, \lambda x: \mathbf{V}_1 . \langle 7, 1 \rangle, \ldots \rangle : \mathbf{V}_\infty$

Objects with a finite number of →s in their type such as

$7: \mathbf{V}_0 \quad \text{succ}: \mathbf{V}_1 \quad \text{twice}: \mathbf{V}_2$

are identified with

$\text{in}_{0,\infty} 7, \quad \text{in}_{1,\infty} \text{succ}, \quad \text{in}_{2,\infty} \text{twice}: \mathbf{V}_\infty$

and so on. Some members of $\mathbf{V}_\infty$, however, only project onto approximations in the $\mathbf{V}_i$:

$f = \lambda g . g\, g \quad f: \mu' u . ' u \to \mathbf{V}_\infty \subseteq \mathbf{V}_\infty$

$p_{\infty,i}\, f = \lambda g: \mathbf{V}_{i-1} . g(p_{i-2} g): \mathbf{V}_i$

Information may be lost by the p_{i-2}.

Because the elements of $\mathbf{V}_\infty$ are tuples, not functions, it is necessary to *define* application in $\mathbf{V}_\infty$.

$v: \mathbf{V}_\infty \quad x: \mathbf{V}_\infty$

$v(x) = \bot \quad \text{if isBv}(v)$

$$= \bigsqcup_{i \geqslant 0} (p_{\infty,i+1} v)(p_{\infty,i} x) \quad \text{otherwise}$$

Each v is an infinite tuple; an element provides some information about v:

$$\text{in}_{i,\infty}(p_{\infty,i} v) \sqsubseteq \text{in}_{i+1,\infty}(p_{\infty,i+1} v) \sqsubseteq v$$

It can be shown [55, 66] that

$$v = \bigsqcup_{i \geqslant 0} p_{\infty,i}(v)$$

Loosely, $\mathbf{V}_\infty$ consists of those infinite tuples whose elements are consistent with each other under the $\text{in}_{i,\infty}$ and $p_{\infty,i}$. $\mathbf{V}_\infty$ is the limit of the $\mathbf{V}_i$ in the sense that $v: \mathbf{V}_\infty$ is the limit of the $\text{in}_{i,\infty}(p_{\infty,i} v)$. v can be treated as a function applied to an element x by 'reading' v one place further right, at i + 1, than x, at i.

Finally **Value** is defined to be $\mathbf{V}_\infty$ with the application operation defined above. This construction provides a model for the untyped λ-calculus with constants.

4.3.3 *Types as ideals*

A typed λ-calculus is a conservative subset of the untyped λ-calculus in that only well-typed expressions are allowed to 'run'. The model of the untyped λ-calculus also provides one for a typed λ-calculus if the types are said to denote certain subsets, *ideals* [33], of the lattice in the model. **Int** denotes the integers and so on. A function type is defined to be

$$S \rightarrow T = \{f \mid x: S \Rightarrow fx: T\}$$

An ideal, T, satisfies

$$\bot : T$$
$$\forall x: T, \forall y, y \sqsubseteq x \Rightarrow y: T$$
$$x_1 \sqsubseteq x_2 \sqsubseteq x_3 \ldots, x_i: T \Rightarrow \sqcup\{x_i\}: T$$

it is 'downwardly closed and upwardly complete'. In particular an ideal is a complete lattice.

Just as λ-expressions are often identified with the functions that they denote, so too type expressions are often identified with the domains that they denote.

4.4 Exercises

1. If $|A| = n$, how many total functions are there from A into A? How many partial functions are there?
2. Show that $|\mathbf{Int}^2| = |\mathbf{Int}|$.
3. Let $f_i(x) = 1 - (1-x)^i$, $\forall i \geqslant 1$, f_i: $[0, 1] \rightarrow [0, 1]$. $\leqslant$ is the usual (total) arithmetic order on $[0, 1]$. Let $\leqslant'$ be the induced partial order on $[0, 1] \rightarrow [0, 1]$. Show that $\langle f_i \rangle$ is an ascending chain of functions. What is the limit function? Show that it is continuous in $[0, 1] \rightarrow [0, 1], \leqslant'$ in the lattice sense.
4. If $\min = \lambda f . f(\bot_{\mathrm{Int}})$ min: $(\mathbf{Int} \rightarrow \mathbf{Int}) \rightarrow \mathbf{Int}$. Show that min is a fixed point operator on $\mathbf{Int} \rightarrow \mathbf{Int}$.
5. Explicitly give the first two or three elements of the tuple in $\mathbf{V}_\infty$ corresponding to each of the following λ-expressions:

   7
   $\mathrm{succ} = \lambda n . n + 1$
   $k = \lambda x, y . x$

5
A simple language

Having seen that even recursive definitions are valid it is now time to give a complete syntactic and semantic definition of a very simple programming language. This definition can be translated into Pascal in an obvious way to give an interpreter. It is hoped that this may appeal to programmers. It also allows experimentation and execution of semantics with no resources other than a Pascal compiler.

5.1 A complete definition

The language to be defined contains integer constants and variables, an assignment, **if** and **while** commands. For control purposes, 0 is used for false and 1 for true. The concrete syntax is given first:

$\gamma ::= \xi := \varepsilon \mid$
 if ε **then** γ **else** $\gamma \mid$
 while ε **do** $\gamma \mid$
 begin γs **end** $\mid$
 skip

$\gamma s ::= \gamma s;\ \gamma \mid \gamma$

$\varepsilon ::= \varepsilon 1 = \varepsilon 1 \mid$
 $\varepsilon 1 < \varepsilon 1 \mid$
 $\varepsilon 1 \leqslant \varepsilon 1 \mid$
 $\varepsilon 1 > \varepsilon 1 \mid$
 $\varepsilon 1 \geqslant \varepsilon 1 \mid$
 $\varepsilon 1 \neq \varepsilon 1 \mid$
 $\varepsilon 1$

$\varepsilon 1 ::= \varepsilon 1 + \varepsilon 2 \mid$
 $\varepsilon 1 - \varepsilon 2 \mid$
 $\varepsilon 2$

$\varepsilon 2 ::= \varepsilon 2 \times \varepsilon 3 \mid$
 $\varepsilon 2 / \varepsilon 3 \mid$
 $\varepsilon 3$

$\varepsilon 3 ::= (\varepsilon) \mid -\varepsilon 3 \mid \nu \mid \xi$

$\nu ::=$ integer constants

$\xi ::=$ syntax for identifiers

This concrete syntax expresses information about the relative binding strength of the operators which is lost in the simpler abstract syntax given below.

Cmd:

$\gamma ::= \xi := \varepsilon \mid$
  if ε **then** γ **else** $\gamma \mid$
  while ε **do** $\gamma \mid$
  $\gamma ; \gamma \mid$
  skip

Exp:

$\varepsilon ::= \varepsilon\ \Omega\ \varepsilon \mid -\varepsilon \mid \nu \mid \xi$

Opr:

$\Omega ::= \; = \mid \neq \mid < \mid > \mid \leqslant \mid \geqslant \mid + \mid - \mid \times \mid /$

The semantics of this programming language can now be given. First the various domains are defined.

σ: **S** = **Ide** → **Int**
Ifns = **Int** × **Int** → **Int**
E: Exp → **S** → **Int**
O: Opr → **Ifns**
C: Cmd → **S** → **S**

The valuation functions **E**, **O** and **C** are defined case by case:

$\mathbf{E}[\![\xi]\!]\sigma = \sigma[\![\xi]\!]$
$\mathbf{E}[\![\nu]\!]\sigma = \mathbf{V}[\![\nu]\!]$
$\mathbf{E}[\![\varepsilon\ \Omega\ \varepsilon']\!]\sigma = \mathbf{O}[\![\Omega]\!]\langle \mathbf{E}[\![\varepsilon]\!]\sigma, \mathbf{E}[\![\varepsilon']\!]\sigma\rangle$
$\mathbf{E}[\![-\varepsilon]\!]\sigma = -\mathbf{E}[\![\varepsilon]\!]\sigma$

$\mathbf{O}[\![+]\!] = + : \mathbf{Int} \times \mathbf{Int} \to \mathbf{Int}$ etc.
$\mathbf{O}[\![<]\!] = \lambda\langle \mathrm{v1}, \mathrm{v2}\rangle .\ \text{if v1} < \text{v2 then 1 else 0}: \mathbf{Int} \times \mathbf{Int} \to \mathbf{Int}$

etc.

$\mathbf{C}[\![\xi := \varepsilon]\!]\sigma = \sigma[\mathbf{E}[\![\varepsilon]\!]\sigma/\xi]$
$\mathbf{C}[\![\textbf{if } \varepsilon \textbf{ then } \gamma \textbf{ else } \gamma']\!]\sigma$
  $= (\text{if } \mathbf{E}[\![\varepsilon]\!]\sigma = 1 \text{ then } \mathbf{C}[\![\gamma]\!] \text{ else } \mathbf{C}[\![\gamma']\!])\sigma$
$\mathbf{C}[\![\textbf{while } \varepsilon \textbf{ do } \gamma]\!]\sigma$
  $= (\text{if } \mathbf{E}[\![\varepsilon]\!]\sigma = 1 \text{ then } \mathbf{C}[\![\textbf{while } \varepsilon \textbf{ do } \gamma]\!] \circ \mathbf{C}[\![\gamma]\!] \text{ else Id})\ \sigma$
$\mathbf{C}[\![\gamma ; \gamma']\!] = \mathbf{C}[\![\gamma']\!] \circ \mathbf{C}[\![\gamma]\!]$
$\mathbf{C}[\![\textbf{skip}]\!] = \mathrm{Id}$

Some of the equations can be written in an equivalent and slightly different way:

$$\mathbf{E}[\![\xi]\!] = \lambda\sigma\,.\,\sigma[\![\xi]\!]$$
$$\mathbf{E}[\![\nu]\!] = \lambda\sigma\,.\,\mathbf{V}[\![\nu]\!]$$

etc.

$$\mathbf{C}[\![\xi := \varepsilon]\!] = \lambda\sigma\,.\,\sigma[\mathbf{E}[\![\varepsilon]\!]\sigma/\xi]$$

etc.

This is because $f(x) = e$ is equivalent to $f = \lambda x\,.\,e$.

These equations can be read in a natural way. The value of a variable, given a state, is the value of the variable in the state. The value of a constant was given in the introduction, § 1.1. The value of an expression consisting of an operator and two subexpressions is the value of the operator (a binary function) applied to the values of the subexpressions. The meaning of an assignment given a state is to update the state, setting the variable to the value of the expression in the state. The meaning of an **if** statement is to use the result of the expression to select the state transformation denoted by either the first or the second substatement to apply to the state. The **while** statement means use the result of the expression to select between applying either the substatement and then the whole **while** statement or just the identity to the state. Sequential execution means apply the second statement to the result of the first statement. The **skip** statement denotes the identity state transformation; it does nothing.

Such English statements may help informal understanding but they are not suitable for formal reasoning about the programming language. English, despite its many charms, is ambiguous and open to interpretation. The formal definition is compact and precise in comparison.

5.2 Examples

The semantic definition can now be applied to some programs to show what they denote.

begin x := 4; y := x + 1 **end**

has the following effect:

$$\begin{aligned}
&\mathbf{C}[\![\textbf{begin}\ x := 4;\ y := x + 1\ \textbf{end}]\!]\sigma\\
&= \mathbf{C}[\![y := x + 1]\!] \circ \mathbf{C}[\![x := 4]\!]\sigma\\
&= \mathbf{C}[\![y := x + 1]\!]\sigma[\mathbf{E}[\![4]\!]\sigma/x]\\
&= \mathbf{C}[\![y := x + 1]\!]\sigma[\mathbf{V}[\![4]\!]/x]\\
&= \mathbf{C}[\![y := x + 1]\!]\sigma[4/x]\\
&= \sigma[4/x,\ \mathbf{E}[\![x + 1]\!]\sigma[4/x]/y]
\end{aligned}$$

$$=\sigma[4/x, \mathbf{O}[\![+]\!]\langle \mathbf{E}[\![x]\!]\sigma[4/x], \mathbf{E}[\![1]\!]\sigma[4/x]\rangle/y]$$
$$=\sigma[4/x, +\langle\sigma[4/x][\![x]\!], \mathbf{V}[\![1]\!]\rangle/y]$$
$$=\sigma[4/x, +\langle 4, 1\rangle/y]$$
$$=\sigma[4/x, 5/y]$$

Whatever is the state σ when the program starts, it finishes with $\sigma[4/x, 5/y]$ as expected. The complete program therefore denotes

$$\lambda\sigma . \sigma[4/x, 5/y]$$

It is extremely unusual to do such calculations in detail and this is not the aim of denotational semantics but it is a useful exercise to gain familiarity with the formulae.

Next consider the program fragment

```
begin f := 1;
      while n>0 do
      begin f := f×n; n := n−1
      end
end
```

Firstly

$$\mathbf{C}[\![f := 1]\!]\sigma = \sigma[1/f]$$

and

$$\mathbf{C}[\![f := f\times n;\ n := n-1]\!]\sigma$$
$$=\sigma[\sigma[\![f]\!]\times\sigma[\![n]\!]/f,\ \sigma[\![n]\!]-1/n]$$

Let the condition $P(\sigma')$ be $\sigma'[\![f]\!]=\sigma[\![n]\!]!/\sigma'[\![n]\!]!$. This certainly holds for $\sigma[1/f]$. If $P(\sigma')$ holds then P holds for

$$\mathbf{C}[\![\textbf{while}\ n>0\ \textbf{do begin}\ f := f\times n;\ n := n-1\ \textbf{end}]\!]\sigma' = \sigma''$$

$\sigma''[\![n]\!]<\sigma'[\![n]\!]$ so if $\sigma[\![n]\!]\geqslant 0$ then the program terminates with state $\sigma[\sigma[\![n]\!]!/f, 0/n]$. If $\sigma[\![n]\!]<0$ then the program does not terminate but in that case $\sigma[\![n]\!]! = \perp$. So the program denotes

$$\lambda\sigma . \sigma[\sigma[\![n]\!]!/f, 0/n].$$

In other words, it calculates n! in f.

5.3 A Pascal translation

The definition given above can be translated directly into standard Pascal, or indeed almost any recursive programming language [3]. The concrete syntax leads to a recursive-descent parser which is not given here. The abstract syntax is used to design a data structure which the parser returns:

```
{syntactic domains}
type exptype =(bexp, {binary operators}
               uexp, {unary operators}
               varr, int);
     opr     =(plus, minus, times, over,
               eq, ne, lt, le, gt, ge, neg);
     cmdtype=(assign, semi, ifstat,
               whiles, skip);
     exp=↑enode;
     enode=record case tag: exptype of
              bexp: (o: opr; left, right: exp);
              uexp: (u: opr; son: exp);
              varr: (id: alfa);
              int: (i: integer)
           end;
     cmd=↑cnode;
     cnode=record case tag: cmdtype of
              assign: (id: alfa; e: exp);
              semi: (left, right: cmd);
              ifstat: (b: exp; gtrue, gfalse: cmd);
              whiles: (bw: exp; g: cmd);
              skip: ( )
           end;
{semantic domains}
Value=integer;
```

The semantic definition of the example language can be coded in standard Pascal by uncurrying the functions.

```
{C: Cmd × S → S}
function C(g: cmd; s: State): State;
begin {main interpreter routine}
  case g↑.tag of
    assign: C:=update(s, g↑.id, E(g↑.e, s));
    semi: C:=C(g↑.right, C(g↑.left, s));
    ifstat: if E(g↑.b, s)=1
              then C:=C(g↑.gtrue, s)
              else C:=C(g↑.gfalse, s);
```

```
      whiles: if E(g↑.bw,s) = 1
                  then C := C(g, C(g↑.g, s))
                  else C := s;
      skip: C := s
    end {case}
  end
```

and

```
  {E: Exp × S → Value}
  function E(e: exp; s: State): Value;
    function O(o: opr; v1, v2: Value): Value;
    begin case o of
            plus: O := v1 + v2;
            etc.
          end {case}
    end {O};
  begin {E}
    case e↑.tag of
      varr: E := applyState(s, e↑.id);
      int: E := e↑.i;
      uexp: E := −E(e↑.son, s) {−only unary op};
      bexp: E := O(e↑.o, E(e↑.left, s), E(e↑.right, s))
    end {case}
  end {E}
```

Note a slight cheat – rather than put the characters of a numeral in the tree and use **V** to calculate the value, the integer value is stored there directly.

One would really like to code a state as a function

```
  function s(id: alfa): Value: . . .
```

and to update it by

```
  {update: S × Ide × Value → S}
  function update(function s: State; id: alfa; val: Value):
    function(id2: alfa): Value;
  begin if id2 = id then update := val else update := s(id2)
  end
```

But this is only possible in a functional programming language. A state is a finite function; it is only defined ($\neq \perp$) on finitely many identifiers. This means a state can be represented by data structure:

```
type State = ↑avar;
     avar = record ident: alfa;
                   v: Value;
                   next: State
            end
```

Such a data structure is often called an association list. It is now easy to update a state in standard Pascal:

```
function update(s: State; id: alfa; val: Value): State;
  var p: State;
begin new(p); p↑.next := s; update := p;
    p↑.ident := id; p↑.v := val
end
```

Note that update produces a new state and does not alter the old one – by overwriting a cell for example.

It is also necessary to write a routine to apply the data structure, State, to a variable:

```
function applyState(s: State; id: alfa): Value;
begin if s = nil
        then applyState := undefined
        else if s↑.ident = id
               then applyState := s↑.v
               else applyState := applyState(s↑.next, id)
end
```

With the concrete syntax coded into a parser returning a data structure corresponding to the abstract syntax, and the semantics coded into an interpreter to walk this data structure, the result is a complete running system.

```
program interpreter(input, output);
label 99;
type State = ... as above ...;
     cmd = ...; exp = ...; as above
function parser: cmd; ...
procedure display (s: State; ... print out state ...;
function undefined: Value;
  begin write(' undefined'); goto 99 end;
function E ... as above ...;
function C ... as above ...;
```

```
begin {main}
   display(C(parser, {startState} = nil));
   99:
end.
```

The complete program is given in the appendix. It is a slow system but it corresponds exactly to the formal definition. This makes it quick to write and one may be very confident that the result is correct. The Pascal compiler checks all of the types in the implementation cum definition which means that a big class of simple mistakes is detected. If the definition is changed, the interpreter can be modified quickly and test programs executed.

5.4 Exercises

1. Extend the semantics of § 5.1 to include

   ε ::= **if** ε **then** ε **else** ε | ... as before
   Ω ::= **and** | **or** | ... as before
   γ ::= **repeat** γ **until** ε |
         if ε **then** γ | ... as before

2. **Project:** use the clauses of Q1 to extend the Pascal interpreter based on the formal semantics.

6
Direct semantics

The language defined in the previous chapter was very simple indeed and lacked several common features. Here side-effects within expressions, declarations, storage allocation, procedures and output are examined. Naturally these features bring certain complications to the semantics but they do not affect the sequence of control in a program, in contrast to **gotos** say (see Ch 7). Therefore the semantics of a compound statement, and in particular of sequential execution (;), can be given *directly* in terms of its component parts. For this reason such semantics are called *direct semantics*.

6.1 Side-effects

Previously the valuation function for expressions had the type

$$\mathbf{E}\colon \mathbf{Exp} \to \mathbf{S} \to \mathbf{Value}$$

$\mathbf{E}[\![\varepsilon]\!]$ was a function from states to values and as such could not modify the state. To broaden this, define

$$\mathbf{E}\colon \mathbf{Exp} \to \mathbf{S} \to \mathbf{Value} \times \mathbf{S}$$

Now $\mathbf{E}[\![\varepsilon]\!]\colon \mathbf{S} \to \mathbf{Value} \times \mathbf{S}$ can return a value and a (possibly) modified state. Assuming syntax as in the previous chapter,

$$\mathbf{E}[\![\xi]\!]\sigma = \langle \sigma[\![\xi]\!], \sigma \rangle$$
$$\mathbf{E}[\![\nu]\!]\sigma = \langle \mathbf{V}[\![\nu]\!], \sigma \rangle$$
$$\mathbf{E}[\![\varepsilon\,\Omega\,\varepsilon']\!]\sigma = \langle \mathbf{O}[\![\Omega]\!]\langle \mathrm{v}, \mathrm{v}' \rangle, \sigma'' \rangle$$
$$\quad \text{where } \langle \mathrm{v}', \sigma'' \rangle = \mathbf{E}[\![\varepsilon']\!]\sigma'$$
$$\quad\quad \text{where } \langle \mathrm{v}, \sigma' \rangle = \mathbf{E}[\![\varepsilon]\!]\sigma$$

The definition of **C** must be changed slightly to accommodate side-effects:

$$\mathbf{C}[\![\xi := \varepsilon]\!]\sigma = \sigma'[\mathrm{v}/\xi]$$
$$\quad \text{where } \langle \mathrm{v}, \sigma' \rangle = \mathbf{E}[\![\varepsilon]\!]\sigma$$
$$\mathbf{C}[\![\mathbf{if}\ \varepsilon\ \mathbf{then}\ \gamma\ \mathbf{else}\ \gamma']\!]\sigma = (\text{if } \mathrm{v} = 1 \text{ then } \mathbf{C}[\![\gamma]\!] \text{ else } \mathbf{C}[\![\gamma']\!])\sigma'$$
$$\quad \text{where } \langle \mathrm{v}, \sigma' \rangle = \mathbf{E}[\![\varepsilon]\!]\sigma$$
$$\mathbf{C}[\![\mathbf{while}\ \varepsilon\ \mathbf{do}\ \gamma]\!]\sigma = (\text{if } \mathrm{v} = 1 \text{ then } \mathbf{C}[\![\mathbf{while} \ldots]\!] \circ \mathbf{C}[\![\gamma]\!] \text{ else Id})\sigma'$$
$$\quad \text{where } \langle \mathrm{v}, \sigma' \rangle = \mathbf{E}[\![\varepsilon]\!]\sigma$$

The possibility of side-effects has forced the order of evaluation of expressions to be specified; here it is left-to-right. There is no avoiding this. In evaluating $\varepsilon\Omega\varepsilon'$, if ε or ε' has a side-effect which alters the state then the result may depend on the order of evaluation. The semantics can say that a certain order is used, or even that there is a choice, but that decision is left to the language designer. Denotational semantics does not say that one choice is better than another.

In fact none of the expression forms given so far allows the possibility of programming a side-effect. What is needed is the ability to execute a command and hence an assignment inside an expression. The simplest form is

Exp:
$\varepsilon ::= \textbf{begin}\ \gamma;\ \varepsilon\ \textbf{end} \mid \ldots$

The intention is that the command γ is executed and then the value of ε is returned, as in the Algol-68 serial-clause:

$$\mathbf{E}[\![\textbf{begin}\ \gamma;\ \varepsilon\ \textbf{end}]\!]\sigma = \mathbf{E}[\![\varepsilon]\!](\mathbf{C}[\![\gamma]\!]\sigma)$$

For example

$$\mathrm{y} := 7;\ \mathrm{x} := \textbf{begin}\ \mathrm{y} := \mathrm{y}+1;\ \mathrm{y}\ \textbf{end}$$

would assign 8 to x and to y under the new definition of **E**.

$$\begin{aligned}
&\mathbf{E}[\![\textbf{begin}\ \mathrm{y} := \mathrm{y}+1;\ \mathrm{y}\ \textbf{end}]\!]\sigma[7/\mathrm{y}]\\
&= \mathbf{E}[\![\mathrm{y}]\!](\mathbf{C}[\![\mathrm{y} := \mathrm{y}+1]\!]\sigma[7/\mathrm{y}])\\
&= \mathbf{E}[\![\mathrm{y}]\!]\sigma[7/\mathrm{y}, (\mathbf{E}[\![\mathrm{y}+1]\!]\sigma[7/\mathrm{y}])_1/\mathrm{y}]\\
&= \mathbf{E}[\![\mathrm{y}]\!]\sigma[7/\mathrm{y}, 8/\mathrm{y}]\\
&= \mathbf{E}[\![\mathrm{y}]\!]\sigma[8/\mathrm{y}]\\
&= \sigma[8/\mathrm{y}][\![\mathrm{y}]\!]\\
&= \langle 8, \sigma[8/\mathrm{y}]\rangle
\end{aligned}$$

and so

$$\begin{aligned}
&\mathbf{C}[\![\mathrm{y} := 7;\ \mathrm{x} := \textbf{begin}\ \mathrm{y} := \mathrm{y}+1;\ \mathrm{y}\ \textbf{end}]\!]\\
&= \lambda\sigma\,.\,\sigma[8/\mathrm{y}, 8/\mathrm{x}]
\end{aligned}$$

6.2 Errors and 'wrong'

In what follows it is necessary to model various error conditions. Just as an extra element, $\perp_D$, was added to each domain D, a further element wrong_D can be added to D to stand for program components that are in error. The partial order, $\sqsubseteq$, satisfies

$$\perp_D \sqsubseteq \mathrm{wrong}_D$$
$$d \text{ and } \mathrm{wrong}_D \quad \text{incomparable if } d \neq \perp_D \text{ and } d \neq \mathrm{wrong}_D$$

The standard functions Cond, o and so on are strict on $\perp$, e.g.

$$\mathrm{Cond}\langle f,g\rangle \perp_{\mathbf{Bool}} = \perp$$

They are also defined to be strict on wrong, e.g.

$$\mathrm{Cond}\langle f,g\rangle \mathrm{wrong}_{\mathbf{Bool}} = \mathrm{wrong}$$

In this way a 'wrong' program stays wrong once it has gone wrong!

6.3 Declarations

The three major components of a programming language such as Pascal are expressions, commands and *declarations*. To declare a named object in a program is to associate the name with some internal machine object. The mapping that does this is called the *environment*. A variable identifier is a name for a location. The *store* maps a location onto its current contents. One name may stand for different objects in different parts of a program. A procedure name stands for the same computation as the procedure body.

6.3.1 *Variables and storage*

In a block-structured language, the scope rule says a variable (or any declared object) is only visible within the block† in which it is declared. An environment, ρ: **Env**, maps the variable identifier onto the object that it denotes or stands for. In a compiled system, a variable identifier stands for a machine location; here an abstraction of locations, **Locn**, is used.

In general there is a range of *denotable values*, **Dv** = **Locn** + ..., that an identifier may stand for. A store maps each location onto its current contents which belongs to the domain of *storable values*, **Sv**. It is usual to define *expressible values*, **Ev**, which expressions may produce. The specifications of **Dv**, **Sv** and **Ev** vary from programming language to programming language; they may overlap or may even be identical and are important characteristics of a language. For example, an identifier may denote an integer (constant) in Pascal but not in Fortran. Booleans may be expressible but not storable in a language where boolean expressions are only used to control conditional commands.

Dec:

$\delta ::= \mathbf{var}\ \xi \mid \delta;\ \delta$

Locn ≡ **Int**

Dv = **Locn** + ...

ρ: **Env** = **Ide** → **Dv** more or less, see below

† In Pascal, block is synonymous with a **procedure** or **function** body. In Algol-68 any structured command is a block.

$$\mathbf{Ev} = \mathbf{Locn} + \mathbf{Int} + \ldots$$

$$\mathbf{Sv} = \mathbf{Int} + \ldots$$
$$\sigma\text{: } \mathbf{Store} = \mathbf{Locn} \to \mathbf{Sv}$$

Cmd:
$$\gamma ::= \mathbf{begin}\ \delta;\ \gamma\ \mathbf{end} \mid \ldots$$

To get the value of a variable ξ is a two-stage process:

$$\sigma(\rho[\![\xi]\!])$$

get the location $\rho[\![\xi]\!]$ bound to ξ and look it up in the store σ. If the variable is not declared $\rho[\![\xi]\!] = \bot_{\mathbf{Dv}}$, and if the variable is declared but uninitialized then $\sigma(\rho[\![\xi]\!]) = \bot_{\mathbf{Ev}}$.

A declaration modifies the current environment and we might give the following types to valuation functions:

$$\mathbf{D}\text{: } \mathbf{Dec} \to \mathbf{Env} \to \mathbf{Env}$$
$$\mathbf{C}\text{: } \mathbf{Cmd} \to \mathbf{Env} \to \mathbf{Store} \to \mathbf{Store}$$
$$\mathbf{E}\text{: } \mathbf{Exp} \to \mathbf{Env} \to \mathbf{Store} \to \mathbf{Ev} \times \mathbf{Store}$$
$$\rho\text{: } \mathbf{Env} = (\mathbf{Ide} \to \mathbf{Dv}) \times \mathbf{Int}$$

$$\mathbf{D}[\![\mathbf{var}\ \xi]\!]\rho = \langle \rho_1[\rho_2/\xi], \rho_2 + 1\rangle$$
$$\mathbf{D}[\![\delta; \delta']\!] = \mathbf{D}[\![\delta']\!] \circ \mathbf{D}[\![\delta]\!]$$
$$\mathbf{C}[\![\mathbf{begin}\ \delta;\ \gamma\ \mathbf{end}]\!]\rho = \mathbf{C}[\![\gamma]\!](\mathbf{D}[\![\delta]\!]\rho)$$
$$\mathbf{C}[\![\xi := \varepsilon]\!]\rho\sigma = \sigma[\mathrm{v}/\rho[\![\xi]\!]]$$
$$\quad \text{where } \langle \mathrm{v}, \sigma\rangle = \mathbf{E}[\![\varepsilon]\!]\rho\sigma$$
$$\mathbf{E}[\![\xi]\!]\rho\sigma = \langle \sigma(\rho[\![\xi]\!]), \sigma\rangle$$

Two identifiers must not stand for the same location within a block, so the environment consists of the mapping as before together with a free-storage counter. When a variable is declared, the variable is *bound* to the free location which is incremented in the new environment.

These semantics give the program

```
begin begin var x; x := 1 end;
      begin var y; y := y + 1 end
end
```

a meaning that is (probably) not intended. The x and y stand for the same location at different times, whereas y should be bound to an uninitialized location.† One way to correct this is to put the free-storage counter in the

† In fact most implementations would do exactly this, but it should not be in the language semantics.

state S of the computation:

$$\mathbf{S} = \mathbf{Int} \times \mathbf{Store}$$
$$\rho\colon \mathbf{Env} = \mathbf{Ide} \to \mathbf{Dv}$$
$$\sigma\colon \mathbf{Store} = \mathbf{Locn} \to \mathbf{Sv}$$

$$\mathbf{D}\colon \mathbf{Dec} \to \mathbf{Env} \to \mathbf{S} \to \mathbf{Env} \times \mathbf{S}$$
$$\mathbf{C}\colon \mathbf{Cmd} \to \mathbf{Env} \to \mathbf{S} \to \mathbf{S}$$
$$\mathbf{E}\colon \mathbf{Exp} \to \mathbf{Env} \to \mathbf{S} \to \mathbf{Ev} \times \mathbf{S}$$

$$\mathbf{D}[\![\mathbf{var}\ \xi]\!]\rho\langle \mathrm{f}, \sigma\rangle = \langle \rho[\mathrm{f}/\xi], \mathrm{f}+1, \sigma\rangle$$
$$\mathbf{D}[\![\delta; \delta']\!] = \mathbf{D}[\![\delta']\!] \circ \mathbf{D}[\![\delta]\!]$$
$$\mathbf{C}[\![\mathbf{begin}\ \delta;\ \gamma\ \mathbf{end}]\!]\rho\langle \mathrm{f}, \sigma\rangle = \mathbf{C}[\![\gamma]\!](\mathbf{D}[\![\delta]\!]\rho\langle \mathrm{f}, \sigma\rangle)$$
$$\mathbf{C}[\![\xi := \varepsilon]\!]\rho\langle \mathrm{f}, \sigma\rangle = \langle \mathrm{f}', \sigma'[\mathrm{v}/\rho[\![\xi]\!]]\rangle$$
$$\quad \text{where } \langle \mathrm{v}, \mathrm{f}', \sigma'\rangle = \mathbf{E}[\![\varepsilon]\!]\rho\langle \mathrm{f}, \sigma\rangle$$
$$\mathbf{E}[\![\xi]\!]\rho\langle \mathrm{f}, \sigma\rangle = \langle \sigma(\rho[\![\xi]\!]), \mathrm{f}, \sigma\rangle$$
$$\mathrm{startenv} = \lambda\xi\,.\,\bot$$
$$\mathrm{startstore} = \lambda \mathrm{l}\,.\,\bot$$

D, **E** and **C** can return a modified free-storage counter and so can change the state that way. As yet no declaration form that can alter the store has been given but some programming languages do have such forms.

6.3.2 *Left and right values*

Many languages allow operations on locations, conditional expressions and a more general form of assignment:

Exp:
$\varepsilon ::= \mathbf{if}\ \varepsilon\ \mathbf{then}\ \varepsilon\ \mathbf{else}\ \varepsilon \mid \ldots$
Cmd:
$\gamma ::= \varepsilon := \varepsilon \mid \ldots$

Recall that this is abstract syntax and can be ambiguous, as indeed it is. The program

$$(\mathbf{if}\ \mathrm{x} < \mathrm{y}\ \mathbf{then}\ \mathrm{x}\ \mathbf{else}\ \mathrm{y}) := \mathbf{if}\ \mathrm{a} > \mathrm{b}\ \mathbf{then}\ \mathrm{a}\ \mathbf{else}\ \mathrm{b}$$

sets the smaller of x and y to the larger of a and b. It is necessary to evaluate an expression differently depending on whether it is to the left or the right of ':='. The expression should yield a *left value* or a location on the left of ':=' and a *right value* or a storable value **Sv** on the right of ':='.

$$\mathbf{E}, \mathbf{L}, \mathbf{R}: \mathbf{Exp} \to \mathbf{Env} \to \mathbf{S} \to \mathbf{Ev} \times \mathbf{S}$$

$$\mathbf{E}[\![\xi]\!]\rho\langle f, \sigma\rangle = \langle \rho[\![\xi]\!], f, \sigma\rangle$$

$$\mathbf{E}[\![\mathbf{if}\ \varepsilon\ \mathbf{then}\ \varepsilon'\ \mathbf{else}\ \varepsilon'']\!]\rho\langle f, \sigma\rangle =$$
$$\quad (\text{if v then } \mathbf{E}[\![\varepsilon']\!] \text{ else } \mathbf{E}[\![\varepsilon'']\!])\rho\langle f', \sigma'\rangle$$
$$\qquad \text{where } \langle v, f', \sigma'\rangle = \mathbf{R}[\![\varepsilon]\!]\rho\langle f, \sigma\rangle$$

$$\mathbf{E}[\![\varepsilon\Omega\varepsilon']\!]\rho\langle f, \sigma\rangle = \langle \mathbf{O}[\![\Omega]\!]\langle v, v'\rangle, f'', \sigma''\rangle$$
$$\quad \text{where } \langle v', f'', \sigma''\rangle = \mathbf{R}[\![\varepsilon']\!]\rho\langle f', \sigma'\rangle$$
$$\qquad \text{where } \langle v, f', \sigma'\rangle = \mathbf{R}[\![\varepsilon]\!]\rho\langle f, \sigma\rangle$$

...

$$\mathbf{R}[\![\varepsilon]\!]\rho\langle f, \sigma\rangle = \text{if isLocn v then } \langle \sigma'(v), f', \sigma'\rangle \text{ else } \langle v, f', \sigma'\rangle$$
$$\qquad \text{where } \langle v, f', \sigma'\rangle = \mathbf{E}[\![\varepsilon]\!]\rho\langle f, \sigma\rangle$$

$$\mathbf{L}[\![\xi]\!]\rho\langle f, \sigma\rangle = \text{if isLocn v then } \langle v, f', \sigma'\rangle \text{ else wrong}$$
$$\quad \text{where } \langle v, f', \sigma'\rangle = \mathbf{E}[\![\varepsilon]\!]\rho\langle f, \sigma\rangle$$

$$\mathbf{C}[\![\varepsilon := \varepsilon']\!]\langle f, \sigma\rangle = \langle f'', \sigma''[v/l]\rangle$$
$$\quad \text{where } \langle v, f'', s''\rangle = \mathbf{R}[\![\varepsilon']\!]\langle f', \sigma'\rangle$$
$$\qquad \text{where } \langle l, f', \sigma'\rangle = \mathbf{L}[\![\varepsilon]\!]\langle f, \sigma\rangle$$

Note that

...; (**if** b **then** 1 **else** 2) := 3

is a 'wrong' program.

6.3.3 *Procedures*

Procedure declaration and call may be given the following syntax:

Dec:

$\delta ::= \mathbf{proc}\ \xi = \gamma \mid \ldots$

Cmd:

$\gamma ::= \xi \mid \ldots$

A procedure value is a state transformation.

$$\mathbf{Proc} = \mathbf{S} \to \mathbf{S}$$
$$\mathbf{Dv} = \mathbf{Locn} + \mathbf{Proc} + \ldots$$

The semantics of a procedure declaration bind an identifier to the computation denoted by the procedure body. This computation should take place, when the procedure is called, in the environment of the place of declaration, not of the call.

$$\mathbf{D}[\![\mathbf{proc}\ \xi = \gamma]\!]\rho\langle f, \sigma\rangle = \langle \rho[p/\xi], f, \sigma\rangle$$
$$\quad \text{where } p = \mathbf{C}[\![\gamma]\!]\rho$$

$$\mathbf{C}[\![\xi]\!]\rho\langle f, \sigma\rangle = \text{if isProc(v) then } v\langle f, \sigma\rangle \text{ else wrong}$$
$$\quad \text{where } v = \rho[\![\xi]\!]$$

The identifier ξ is bound to p: **Proc** which incorporates the environment from the declaration of the procedure. It must also be checked that the identifier in a call really is bound to a **Proc**. This is rudimentary type checking. Similarly, **E** must produce an **Ev**:

$$\mathbf{E}[\![\xi]\!]\rho\langle \mathrm{f}, \sigma\rangle = \text{if isLocn(v) then } \langle \mathrm{v}, \mathrm{f}, \sigma\rangle \text{ else wrong}$$
$$\text{where } \mathrm{v} = \rho[\![\xi]\!]$$

The rule given above does not allow recursive procedures, for the procedure body is executed in an environment which does not include the binding of the procedure identifier to that body. To rectify this, use

$$\mathbf{D}[\![\mathbf{proc}\ \xi = \gamma]\!]\rho\langle \mathrm{f}, \sigma\rangle = \langle \rho', \mathrm{f}, \sigma\rangle$$
$$\text{where } \rho' = \rho[\mathrm{p}/\xi]$$
$$\text{and } \mathrm{p} = \mathbf{C}[\![\gamma]\!]\rho'$$

Note that the modified environment, ρ', is defined recursively in terms of itself. This rule allows self-recursive procedures and mutually recursive procedures provided one is defined inside the other, in the style of Pascal without **forward** declarations.

The program

```
begin proc p = begin .... ; q; .... end;
      proc q = begin .... ; p; .... end;
   p
end
```

will not run as q is undefined within p. The easiest way to extend the semantics to allow this program to run is to use the abstract syntax:

Dec:

$\delta ::= \mathbf{proc}\ \xi^+ = \gamma^+ \mid \ldots$

where the lengths of the list of identifiers and the list of commands are the same and ξ_1 is associated with γ_1 and so on.

$$\mathbf{D}[\![\mathbf{proc}\ \xi_1, \ldots, \xi_n = \gamma_1, \ldots, \gamma_n]\!]\rho\langle \mathrm{f}, \sigma\rangle = \langle \rho', \mathrm{f}, \sigma\rangle$$
$$\text{where } \rho' = \rho[\mathrm{p}_1/\xi_1, \ldots, \mathrm{p}_n/\xi_n]$$
$$\text{where } \mathrm{p}_1 = \mathbf{C}[\![\gamma_1]\!]\rho'$$
$$\ldots$$
$$\mathrm{p}_n = \mathbf{C}[\![\gamma_n]\!]\rho'$$

The parser may allow any desired concrete syntax provided that it is translated into the given abstract syntax.

6.3.4 *Functions*

Functions follow the definition of procedures straightforwardly producing a value as well as a state:

Dec:

func $\xi = \varepsilon$

Exp:

$\varepsilon ::= \xi(\,) \mid \ldots$ function call

Func = **S** → **Ev** × **S**

Dv = **Func** + ...

$\mathbf{D}[\![\mathbf{func}\ \xi = \varepsilon]\!]\rho\langle \mathrm{f}, \sigma\rangle = \langle \rho', \mathrm{f}, \sigma\rangle$
  where $\rho' = \rho[\mathrm{f}/\xi]$
  and $\mathrm{f} = \lambda\langle \mathrm{f}, \sigma\rangle . \mathbf{E}[\![\varepsilon]\!]\rho'\langle \mathrm{f}, \sigma\rangle$

$\mathbf{E}[\![\xi(\,)]\!]\rho\langle \mathrm{f}, \sigma\rangle = \text{if isFunc(v) then } \mathrm{v}\langle \mathrm{f}, \sigma\rangle \text{ else wrong}$
  where $\mathrm{v} = \rho[\![\xi]\!]$

6.3.5 *Parameters*

There are two aspects to passing a parameter – evaluating the actual parameter and binding it to the formal parameter. This binding is like a declaration:

Cmd:

$\gamma ::= \xi(\varepsilon) \mid \ldots$

Dec:

$\delta ::= \mathbf{proc}\ \xi(\xi) = \gamma \mid \ldots$

Procl = **Ev** → **Proc**

$\mathbf{D}[\![\mathbf{proc}\ \xi(\xi') = \gamma]\!]\rho\langle \mathrm{f}, \sigma\rangle = \langle \rho', \mathrm{f}, \sigma\rangle$
  where $\rho' = \rho[\mathrm{p}/\xi]$
    where $\mathrm{p} = \lambda \mathrm{l}, \langle \mathrm{f}, \sigma\rangle . \text{ if isLocn(l)}$
      $\text{then } \mathbf{C}[\![\gamma]\!]\rho'[\mathrm{l}/\xi']\langle \mathrm{f}, \sigma\rangle$
      else wrong

$\mathbf{C}[\![\ \xi(\varepsilon)\ ]\!]\rho\langle \mathrm{f}, \sigma\rangle = \text{if isProc1(v) then v l } \langle \mathrm{f}, \sigma'\rangle \text{ else wrong}$
  where $\mathrm{v} = \rho[\![\xi]\!]$
  and $\mathrm{l}, \mathrm{f}', \sigma' = \mathbf{E}[\![\varepsilon]\!]\rho\langle \mathrm{f}, \sigma\rangle$

The declaration binds p: **Procl** to ξ as before – §6.3.3. The body of the procedure, γ, is executed in an environment $\rho'[\mathrm{l}/\xi']$ that binds some location, l, to the formal parameter ξ'. This defines passing a parameter *by-reference*. It is the mechanism of Pascal's **var** parameter.

The definition of *by-value* parameter passing is left as an exercise.

A parameter is passed *by-name* by replacing the formal parameter throughout the procedure body with the corresponding actual parameter:

$$\mathbf{C}[\![\xi(\varepsilon)]\!]\rho\langle f,\sigma\rangle = \text{if isProc1(v) then v t } \langle f,\sigma\rangle$$
$$\text{where } t = \mathbf{E}[\![\varepsilon]\!]\rho : \mathbf{S} \to \mathbf{Ev} \times \mathbf{S} = \mathbf{Func}$$
$$\text{and } v = \rho[\![\xi]\!]$$

so $\mathbf{Proc1} = \mathbf{Func} \to \mathbf{Proc}$

t is called a *closure* or a *thunk*. It is an implicit function whose result is the actual parameter. That result may depend on the current state. No name clashes are possible because the environment used in t is fixed as ρ from the call, and that used in the procedure body comes from its declaration.

Adding parameters to functions follows a similar pattern.

The domain of procedures of more than one parameter can be modelled by

$$\mathbf{Proc}_* = (\mathbf{Ev} \to \mathbf{Proc}_*) + \mathbf{Proc}$$

or by

$$\mathbf{Proc}_* = \mathbf{Ev}^+ \to \mathbf{Proc}$$

Checking the number and kind of the actual parameters is straightforward.

6.4 Output

Not since the days of the Manchester Mk1 has a store image been used as the standard means of receiving the output of a program. The output file can be modelled in the following way:

$$\mathbf{Ans} = \{\text{nil}\} + \mathbf{Bv} \times \mathbf{Ans}$$
$$\mathbf{Bv} = \mathbf{Int} + \ldots$$

$$\mathbf{S} = \mathbf{Int} \times \mathbf{Store} \times \mathbf{Ans}$$

Cmd:

$\gamma ::= \text{write } \varepsilon \mid \ldots$

$$\mathbf{C}[\![\text{write } \varepsilon]\!]\rho\langle f,\sigma,a\rangle = \text{if isBv v then } \langle f',\sigma',\text{append}(a',v)\rangle \text{ else wrong}$$
$$\text{where } \langle v,f',\sigma',a'\rangle = \mathbf{R}[\![\varepsilon]\!]\rho\langle f,\sigma,a\rangle$$

The output, or answer **Ans**, of the program is a list of basic values **Bv**. An extra component, **Ans**, is added to the state of the computation. The write command evaluates an expression, checks that it is printable, and appends it to the output. Other clauses of **C**, **E** and **D**, are trivially modified to handle the output as part of the state.

The program

while 1 = 1 **do** write 1

produces an infinite output when executed. If the semantic equations are viewed as an interpreter, as in §6.5, they should be understood to be executed in normal order otherwise the above program will be undefined because it does not terminate.

An input file can easily be added as an extra component to **S**, together with a read command to **Cmd**, or a read expression to **Exp**.

6.5 A Pascal translation

The semantics given in this chapter can be translated into Pascal, although with more reservations than before. It still allows many interesting experiments to be carried out. For simplicity, only parameterless procedures are covered.

The store and environment are both finite functions and can be represented by data structures, such as linked lists. **E**, **D** and **C** return direct products which is not allowed in Pascal, but a pointer to a record which contains the components *can* be returned. As there is no pattern-matching form of function definition, components of products must be explicitly extracted by the use of '↑', '.' and field identifiers. The lack of polymorphic types means that several essentially equivalent functions must be defined.

The syntactic domains are slightly extended:

```
type {some omitted}
    exp = ↑ enode;
    enode = record case tag: exptype of
            bexp: (o: opr; left, right: exp);
            uexp: (u: opr; son: exp);
            varr: (id: alfa);
            int:  (i: integer);
            ifexp: (e1, e2, e3: exp)
          end;
    cmd = ↑ cnode;
    dec = ↑ dnode;
    dnode = record case tag: dectypes of
            declist:  (left, right: dec);
            vardec:   (vid: alfa);
            procdec:  (id: alfa; g: cmd)
          end;
    cnode = record case tag: cmdtype of
            block:  (d: dec; body: cmd);
            call:   (pid: alfa);
            assign: (lhs, e: exp);
            semi:   (left, right: cmd);
            ifstat: (b: exp; gtrue, gfalse: cmd);
            whiles: (bw: exp; g: cmd);
            writte: (op: exp);
            skip:   ( )
          end;
```

The semantic domains follow, environments and stores being coded as lists:

```
Locn = integer;
valtype = (isInt, isLocn, isProc);
Ev = ↑Evrec;          {Ev = Locn + Int - expressible values}
Evrec = record case tag: valtype of
                isLocn: (l: Locn);
                isInt: (i: integer)
        end;
Answer = ↑ansrec;     {Answer = integer↑* - answers or output}
ansrec = record v: integer;     {Bv = Int}
               next: Answer
        end;
Store = ↑storec;      {Store = Ide → Ev}
storec = record l: Locn;
               v: Ev;     {Sv = Ev}
               next: Store
        end;
State = ↑starec;      {State = Int × Store × Answer}
starec = record free: integer;
               sto: Store;
               ans: Answer
        end;
Dv = ↑Dvrec;          {Dv = Locn + Proc}
Env = ↑envrec;        {Env = Ide → Dv}
Dvrec = record case tag: valtype of
                isLocn: (l: Locn);
                isProc: (body: cmd; e: Env)
        end;
envrec = record id: alfa;
               binding: Dv;
               next: Env
        end;
```

Note that **Proc** = **S** → **S** in the semantics, but a function cannot be stored in a Pascal data structure. Therefore a **Proc** must be coded as a **Cmd** × **Env** in the **Env** data structure. When the **Proc** is called, the command is executed with the stored environment.

It is necessary to define the direct products returned by **E**, **D** and **C**:

```
Env × State = ↑e × srec;
e × srec = record e: Env; s: State end;
Ev × State = ↑ev × srec;
ev × srec = record v: Ev; s: State end;
```

A number of auxiliary functions are needed:

```
procedure display(s: State);   {print answer etc.}
function consSta(f: integer; s: Store; a: Answer): State;
  var p: State;
begin new(p); consSta := p;
    with p↑ do begin free := f; sto := s; ans := a end
end;
function pairEnvSta(e: Env; s: State): Env × State;   {similar to above}
function pairEvSta(v: Ev; s: State): Ev × State;   {ditto}
```

Injection into direct sums is not implicit so explicit functions are needed. It can be argued that this is a good thing as it makes the writer more careful.

```
function LocnDv(l: Locn): Dv;
  var p: Dv;
begin new(p); LocnDv := p;
     p↑.tag := isLocn; p↑.l := l
end;
function ProcDv(e: Env; g: cmd): Dv; {see above}
function IntEv(i: integer): Ev; {ditto}
function LocnEv(l: Locn): Ev; {ditto}
function undefEv: Ev;
  {not a function in the semantics; a fn here for side-effect of stop}
  begin error('run: undfEv') end;
function undefDv: Dv; {see above}
procedure wrong; {run time errors}
begin error('run: wrong') end;
```

The store, and now the environment, are manipulated as before in Ch 5.

```
function updateSto(s: Store; l: Locn; val: Ev): Store;
function applySto(s: Store; l: Locn): Ev; {ditto}
function reserve(s: State): State;
  var p: State;
begin new(p);
     p↑ := s↑; p↑.free := p↑.free + 1; reserve := p
end;
```

```
function updateEnv(e: Env; id: alfa; b: Dv): Env;
  var newe: Env;
begin new(newe); newe↑.next := e; updateEnv := newe;
      newe↑.id := id; newe↑.binding := b
end;
```

To allow recursive procedures, a procedure body must be executed in the environment current where the procedure is declared. Examination of YEnv, **D** applied to procedures and **C** applied to calls will reveal how this is ensured.

```
function YEnv(e: Env): Env;
{ for a recursive function }
begin e↑.binding↑.e := e;   YEnv := e   end;

function applyEnv(e: Env; id: alfa): Dv;
begin if e = nil
        then applyEnv := undefDv {undeclared identifier}
        else if e↑.id = id
               then applyEnv := e↑.binding
               else applyEnv := applyEnv(e↑.next, id)
end;
```

Note that, because Pascal most definitely does not use normal-order evaluation, programs that produce infinite output are not defined by this interpreter.

```
function appendAns(a: Answer; v: Ev): Answer; { =a+ +v}
function L(e: exp; e×s: Env×State): Ev×State; forward;
function R(e: exp; e×s: Env×State): Ev×State; forward;
  {: Exp×Env×State → Ev×State }
function E(e: exp; e×s: Env×State): Ev×State;
  var denv: Dv; v×st: Ev×State;
      v1×s1, v2×s2: Ev×State;
  function O(o: opr; v1, v2: Ev): Ev; {: opr×Ev×Ev → Ev }
    var i1, i2: integer;
  begin if (v1↑.tag≠isInt) or (v2↑.tag≠isInt)
        then wrong
        else
        begin i1 := v1↑.i; i2 := v2↑.i;
          case o of
            plus: O := IntEv(i1+i2);
              ...etc...
          end {case}
        end
  end {O};
```

```
begin {E}
  case e↑.tag of
    varr: begin denv := applyEnv(e×s↑.e, e↑.id);
               case denv↑.tag of
                 isLocn: E := pairEvSta(LocnEv(denv↑.l), e×s↑.s);
                 isProc: wrong
               end
          end;
    int:  E := pairEvSta(IntEv(e↑.i), e×s↑.s);
    uexp: ...
    bexp: begin v1×s1 := R(e↑.left, e×s);
               v2×s2 := R(e↑.right, pairEnvSta(e×s↑.e, v1×s1↑.s));
               E := pairEvSta( O(e↑.o, v1×s1↑.v, v2×s2↑.v),
                                                    v2×s2↑.s)
          end;
    ifexp:...
  end {case}
end {E};
function L;      {: exp × Env × State → Ev × State }
  var v×s: Ev × State;
begin v×s := E(e, e×s);
      case v×s↑.v↑.tag of
        isInt: wrong;
        isLocn: L := v×s
      end
end;
function R;      {: exp × Env × State → Ev × State }
  var v×s: Ev × State; contents: Ev;
begin v×s := E(e, e×s);
      case v×s↑.v↑.tag of
        isInt: R := v×s;
        isLocn: begin contents := applySto(v×s↑.s↑.sto, v×s↑.v↑.l);
                      R := pairEvSta(contents, v×s↑.s)
                end
      end
end;
```

Function **D** processes declarations:

```
function D(d: dec; e×s: Env×State): Env×State;
begin if d=nil
        then D:=e×s {block may have no declns}
        else case d↑.tag of
                declist: {d1; d2}D:=D(d↑.right, D(d↑.left, e×s));
                vardec: {var x}
                  D:=pairEnvSta(updateEnv(e×s↑.e, d↑.vid,
                                          LocnDv(e×s↑.s↑.free)),
                                reserve(e×s↑.s));
                procdec: {proc id=g   fixed-pt for recursive procs}
                  D:=pairEnvSta(YEnv(updateEnv(e×s↑.e, d↑.id,
                                          ProcDv(nil{Y}, d↑.g))),
                                e×s↑.s)
              end
end;
{State=Int×Store×Answer}
function C(g: cmd; e×s: Env×State): State;
           {: Cmd×Env×State→State}
  var denv: Dv; v1×s1, v2×s2: Ev×State;
begin {Main interpreter routine}
  case g↑.tag of
    block: C:=C(g↑.body, D(g↑.d, e×s));
    call:  begin denv:=applyEnv(e×s↑.e, g↑.pid);
             case denv↑.tag of
               isLocn: wrong;
               isProc:
                 C:=C(denv↑.body,
                      pairEnvSta(denv↑.e, e×s↑.s))
             end
           end;
    semi:  C:=C(g↑.right, pairEnvSta(e×s↑.e, C(g↑.left, e×s)) );
    ifstat: ...
    assign: ...
    whiles: ...
    writte: begin v1×s1:=R(g↑.op, e×s);
             C:=consSta(v1×s1↑.s↑.free, v1×s1↑.s↑.sto,
                  appendAns(v1×s1↑.s↑.ans, v1×s1↑.v))
           end;
    skip:  C:=e×s↑.s
  end {case}
end {C};
```

```
begin
  new(startState);
  with startState↑ do
    begin free:=0; sto:=nil; ans:=nil end;
  display( C(parser, pairEnvSta({Env=}nil, startState) ) );
  99: {fin}
end.
```

6.6 Exercises

1. Give semantics for the declaration of constants:

   Dec:
   δ ::= **const** $\xi = \varepsilon$ | ...

   There are two principal variations:
   (a) restrict ε to compile-time expressions or even literals, as in Pascal;
   (b) allow arbitrary expressions, with side-effects and so on, which is more like Algol-68.

2. Use 1(b) as a guide to the definition of by-value parameter passing. There are two principal variations. In Pascal a value formal parameter is a variable which is initialized to the actual parameter's value at the call. In Algol-68 the formal parameter is bound to the value of the actual parameter and cannot change during the procedure's execution.

3. Define the use of undeclared identifiers to be 'wrong' rather than undefined, $\perp$.

4. Redefine the semantics of §6.3.3 to include **Proc** in **Ev**, but not in **Sv**, so that the following is allowed:

   Cmd:
   γ ::= ε | ... a call

5. Modify the semantics of §6.4 to include an input file and

   Exp:
   ε ::= read | ...

6. **Project:** modify the Pascal translation given in §6.5 to include some or all of the above.

7
Control

Commands that cause transfers of control are called *sequencers*. Examples are **goto**, **return**, **exit**, **resultis**, **break** and **continue**. The desirability or danger of such features is hotly debated in the literature. Here it will just be shown how they can be defined denotationally. To do this it is necessary to introduce function domains called continuations. A good understanding of high-order functions is needed to master this area; see Ch 3.

Sequencers can affect the execution of expressions and declarations as well as commands. This necessitates widespread changes to the semantics which are introduced in gradual stages.

7.1 Control commands

Recall that sequential execution was defined by

$$\mathbf{C}[\![\gamma;\gamma']\!]=\mathbf{C}[\![\gamma']\!]\circ\mathbf{C}[\![\gamma]\!]$$

γ and γ' are arbitrary commands, even **goto**s if we have

Cmd:

γ ::= **goto** ϕ | ....

Labels:

ϕ ::= syntax for labels

In that case

$$\begin{aligned}&\mathbf{C}[\![\mathbf{goto}\ \phi;\gamma]\!]\sigma\\&=\mathbf{C}[\![\gamma]\!]\circ\mathbf{C}[\![\mathbf{goto}\ \phi]\!]\sigma\\&=\mathbf{C}[\![\gamma]\!](\mathbf{C}[\![\mathbf{goto}\ \phi]\!]\sigma)\end{aligned}$$

so the result depends on γ. But this is not what **goto**s do. The whole point of such a jump is that γ is avoided. Somehow $\mathbf{C}[\![\gamma]\!]$ should be discarded from the right-hand side of the equation in this case. The only way to do this is (approximately) to make $\mathbf{C}[\![\gamma']\!]$ a parameter to $\mathbf{C}[\![\gamma]\!]$ in $\mathbf{C}[\![\gamma;\gamma']\!]$ so that $\mathbf{C}[\![\gamma]\!]$ can discard $\mathbf{C}[\![\gamma']\!]$ if γ is a **goto**. A second problem is to decide what labels denote.

A label is some point in the program where computation will continue if the label is jumped to. A computation is a state transformation $\mathbf{S} \to \mathbf{S}$ and this is what labels stand for. For reasons that will become obvious such computations are called (command) *continuations* $\mathbf{Cont} = \mathbf{S} \to \mathbf{S}$. Lastly the environment must contain a component to map labels onto their denotations:

$$\rho: \mathbf{Env} = \mathbf{Labels} \to \mathbf{Cont}$$

To keep matters simple, a small language with a **goto** command but without side-effects in expressions follows in the style of Strachey and Wadsworth [61]:

Cmd:
$\gamma ::= \xi := \varepsilon \mid$
- **if** ε **then** γ **else** $\gamma \mid$
- **while** ε **do** $\gamma \mid$
- $\gamma; \gamma \mid$
- **skip** $\mid$
- **begin** γ **end** $\mid$
- $\phi: \gamma \mid$ labelled command
- **goto** ϕ

Labels:
$\phi ::=$ syntax for labels

Exp:
$\varepsilon ::= \varepsilon\ \Omega\ \varepsilon \mid -\varepsilon \mid \nu \mid \xi$

Opr:
$\Omega ::= \; = \mid \neq \mid < \mid > \mid \leqslant \mid \geqslant \mid + \mid - \mid \times \mid /$

Note that illegal multiple definitions of a label are best forbidden by context-sensitive syntax.

The semantics of this language are given by

$\mathbf{E}: \mathbf{Exp} \to \mathbf{S} \to \mathbf{Value}$ as before, Ch 5
$\mathbf{O}: \mathbf{Opr} \to \mathbf{Ifns}$ as before
$\theta: \mathbf{Cont} = \mathbf{S} \to \mathbf{S}$
$\rho: \mathbf{Env} = \mathbf{Labels} \to \mathbf{Cont}$
$\mathbf{P}: \mathbf{Cmd} \to \mathbf{Env} \to \mathbf{Cont} \to \mathbf{S} \to \mathbf{S}$

$$\mathbf{P}[\![\xi := \varepsilon]\!]\rho\theta\sigma = \theta\sigma[\mathbf{E}[\![\varepsilon]\!]\sigma/\xi]$$
$$\mathbf{P}[\![\textbf{if } \varepsilon \textbf{ then } \gamma \textbf{ else } \gamma']\!]\rho\theta\sigma = (\text{if } \mathbf{E}[\![\varepsilon]\!]\sigma = 1 \text{ then } \mathbf{P}[\![\gamma]\!] \text{ else } \mathbf{P}[\![\gamma']\!])\rho\theta\sigma$$
$$\mathbf{P}[\![\textbf{while } \varepsilon \textbf{ do } \gamma]\!]\rho\theta\sigma = (\text{if } \mathbf{E}[\![\varepsilon]\!]\sigma = 1 \text{ then } \mathbf{P}[\![\gamma]\!]\rho\{\mathbf{P}[\![\textbf{while} \ldots]\!]\rho\theta\} \text{ else } \theta)\sigma$$
$$\mathbf{P}[\![\gamma; \gamma']\!]\rho\theta\sigma = \mathbf{P}[\![\gamma]\!]\rho\{\mathbf{P}[\![\gamma']\!]\rho\theta\}\sigma$$
$$\mathbf{P}[\![\textbf{skip}]\!]\rho\theta\sigma = \theta(\sigma)$$

$$\begin{aligned}
&\mathbf{P}[\![\textbf{begin}\ \phi_1 : \gamma_1,\ \sigma_2 : \gamma_2;\ \ldots\ \phi_n : \gamma_n\ \textbf{end}]\!]\rho\theta = \theta_1\\
&\qquad \text{where } \theta_1 = \mathbf{P}[\![\gamma_1]\!]\rho'\theta_2\\
&\qquad\qquad\quad \theta_2 = \mathbf{P}[\![\gamma_2]\!]\rho'\theta_3\\
&\qquad\qquad\quad \ldots\\
&\qquad\qquad\quad \theta_n = \mathbf{P}[\![\gamma_n]\!]\rho'\theta\\
&\qquad \text{and} \quad \rho' = \rho[\theta_1/\phi_1, \ldots \theta_n/\phi_n]\\
&\mathbf{P}[\![\textbf{goto}\ \phi]\!]\rho\theta\sigma = \rho[\![\phi]\!]\sigma\\
&\mathbf{P}[\![\phi : \gamma]\!] = \mathbf{P}[\![\gamma]\!]
\end{aligned}$$

It is traditional to use **P** rather than to redefine **C** because the requirements of continuations have transformed the semantics quite significantly. The continuation θ: **Cont** that appears in the rules can be thought of as 'something to do after' the command being defined 'in normal circumstances'. The type of **P** includes an environment because this is needed to interpret any labels within commands.

It makes the semantics simpler to pretend that all commands within a compound command, **begin** ... **end**, are labelled. A parser could arrange this by inserting dummy labels and using the rule $\gamma ::= \gamma ; \gamma$ to group unlabelled commands.

The rule for $\mathbf{P}[\![\textbf{begin}\ \phi_i : \gamma_i\ \textbf{end}]\!]$ defines both the meaning of labels and their scope. A label name can be redefined in an inner compound command and, during that command, jumps refer to the inner definition. It is therefore not possible to jump into a compound command which is a common restriction in programming languages with **gotos**.

It can be seen that the standard control mechanism of this language is sequential execution. To execute a compound command, execute the first command and then θ_2. To execute θ_2, execute the second command and so on. Eventually leave the compound command and execute its continuation, θ. That is provided none of the sub-commands cause a jump to be executed. The definition of the θ_is is potentially recursive because the γ_is may refer to them. This should not be surprising because it is possible to program the effect of **while** loops with **if** and **goto** commands.

The definition of $\gamma; \gamma'$ can be read as, to execute $\gamma; \gamma'$ in an environment ρ with a continuation θ and store σ, execute γ in environment ρ with continuation θ' and store σ, where θ' is execute γ' in environment ρ with continuation θ. It is usual to enclose complex continuations in braces { }, as in $\{\mathbf{P}[\![\gamma']\!]\rho\theta\}$, to emphasize their limits; there is no great significance in this as it is just a visual aid. The store that θ' is applied to will come from $\mathbf{P}[\![\gamma]\!]$. However, if γ is a **goto** or contains a **goto**, it is possible that θ' will never be invoked. Note that γ and γ' appear in the same order on the right-hand side as on the left-hand side of the definition. More informally still, the definition can be read as, to do $\gamma;\gamma'$ and then θ, do γ and then do γ' and finally θ.

The definition of **goto** is the most interesting:

$$\mathbf{P}[\![\mathbf{goto}\ \phi]\!]\rho\theta\sigma = \rho[\![\phi]\!]\sigma$$

To execute **goto** ϕ in environment ρ and then do θ all with state σ, look up ϕ in the environment and apply the resulting continuation $\rho[\![\phi]\!]$ to σ. Note that θ has been dropped on the right-hand side of the definition. It does not matter what textually follows the **goto**, it will not be executed in general.

$$\begin{aligned}&\mathbf{P}[\![\mathbf{goto}\ \phi;\ \gamma]\!]\rho\theta\sigma\\ &= \mathbf{P}[\![\mathbf{goto}\ \phi]\!]\rho\{\mathbf{P}[\![\gamma]\!]\rho\theta\}\sigma\\ &= \rho[\![\phi]\!]\sigma\end{aligned}$$

Owing to the way that the environment ρ is updated in compound commands, a use of label ϕ will always refer to the innermost definition of ϕ. If there is *no* matching label definition then $\rho[\![\phi]\!] = \bot$: **Cont** the undefined continuation and the program is undefined.

7.2 More continuations

In case continuations have proved hard to understand some examples will be given. The return address to any procedure or function is a continuation – it is a point at which computation continues or resumes when the procedure finishes under normal circumstances. The procedure might, however, execute a jump to some other point in the program and discard its normal continuation. In implementations, the return address is always passed as an invisible parameter to the called procedure; it is stored in the linkage area.

Suppose one were doing some calculations on real numbers:

sqrt, exp: **Real** → **Real**

exp ∘ sqrt: **Real** → **Real** is a function which exponentiates the square root of its parameter. But, if $x<0$, sqrt(x) = $\bot$: **Real**, and so also exp ∘ srqt(x) = $\bot$: **Real**. There is no possibility to take emergency action in sqrt in the abnormal circumstance that $x<0$.

However, if we define

Rcont = **Real** → **Real**

sqrt′ = λf, x . if $x<0$ then emergency calculation else f(sqrt(x))

Then, if $x \geqslant 0$, sqrt′exp x = exp ∘ sqrt x, but if $x<0$ then sqrt′ can take appropriate action. Note that if we had just defined

$\text{sqrt}'' : \mathbf{Real} \rightarrow \mathbf{Real}$

$\text{sqrt}'' = \lambda x\,.\,\text{if } x<0 \text{ then emergency calculation}'' \text{ else sqrt}(x)$

and used exp∘sqrt″, there is no way that sqrt″ could use exp in its emergency calculation because it has no access to it. sqrt′, however, can use exp, or whatever follows sqrt′, in its emergency calculation because it has access to exp via parameter f.

This can be a useful technique in functional programming. There are generalizations in which a function can be given two continuations – a normal one and a continuation for certain anticipated error conditions – and so on.

7.3 Output and answers

The use of continuations permits a very neat treatment of output and program termination conditions. Recall, §6.4, that an answer was a list of printable or basic values. We can give a slightly different definition:

$\mathbf{Ans} = \{\text{wrong}, \text{finish}\} + \mathbf{Bv} \times \mathbf{Ans}$

$\mathbf{Bv} = \mathbf{Int} + \ldots$

An answer is a possibly infinite list of basic values, but if the list is finite then it terminates in either 'wrong' or 'finish'. The former indicates a program that has crashed and the latter one that has terminated normally.

A continuation or computation is defined to take a state and produce an answer:

$\mathbf{Cont} = \mathbf{S} \rightarrow \mathbf{Ans}$

The value of a variable is not part of the answer; it is inaccessible to the programmer when the program has stopped. Only the written output is returned. A continuation may run forever and return a possibly infinite output list, or terminate wrongly or finish normally.

Cmd:

$\gamma ::= \text{write } \varepsilon \mid \ldots$

$\mathbf{P}: \mathbf{Cmd} \rightarrow \mathbf{Env} \rightarrow \mathbf{Cont} \rightarrow \mathbf{S} \rightarrow \mathbf{Ans}$

$\mathbf{P}[\![\text{write } \varepsilon]\!]\rho\theta\sigma = \langle v, \theta\sigma \rangle$

$\quad \text{where } v = \mathbf{E}[\![\varepsilon]\!]\sigma$

For the rest, the definition of **P** follows that given above in §7.1.

7.4 Side-effects and sequencers

If expressions can have side-effects by the execution of commands and in particular assignments, then any sequencers in the language can also be executed within an expression. This can cause a jump right out of an expression and can prevent a value ever being calculated by it. As might be expected, this requires major surgery on **E** which defines expressions. At the same time it becomes possible to define sequencers specific to expressions, and the **valof–resultis** [61] construction is one.

It is necessary to define *expression kontinuations*, **Kont**. An expression kontinuation κ: **Kont** takes or uses the value produced by an expression. The continuation for the expression in an **if** command uses the value to select one of the arms of the **if** to execute. The continuation of the expression in an assignment uses the value to update the state.

Another programming language based on those defined previously (see §6.1), excluding declarations but including side-effects and sequencers, is given below:

Cmd:

$\gamma ::= \xi := \varepsilon \mid$
  if ε **then** γ **else** $\gamma \mid$
  while ε **do** $\gamma \mid$
  $\gamma; \gamma \mid$
  skip $\mid$
  begin $\phi_i : \gamma_i$ **end** $\mid$
  $\phi : \gamma \mid$
  write $\varepsilon \mid$
  resultis $\varepsilon \mid$
  goto ϕ

Labels:

$\phi ::=$ syntax of labels

Exp:

$\varepsilon ::= \varepsilon\ \Omega\ \varepsilon \mid -\varepsilon \mid \nu \mid \xi \mid$ **valof** γ

Opr:

$\Omega ::= \; = \mid \neq \mid < \mid > \mid \leqslant \mid \geqslant \mid + \mid - \mid * \mid /$

The domains and the types of the valuation functions are:

σ: **S = Ide → Value**
ρ: **Env = (Labels → Cont) × Kont**
θ: **Cont = S → Ans**
κ: **Kont = Value → S → Ans**
E: Exp → Env → Kont → S → Ans
P: Cmd → Env → Cont → S → Ans
O: Opr → Ifns

The new definition of **E** is as follows:

$$\mathbf{E}[\![v]\!]\rho\kappa=\kappa(\mathbf{V}[\![v]\!])$$
$$\mathbf{E}[\![\xi]\!]\rho\kappa\sigma=\kappa(\sigma[\![\xi]\!])$$
$$\mathbf{E}[\![\mathbf{valof}\ \gamma]\!]\rho\kappa=\mathbf{P}[\![\gamma]\!]\rho'\{\text{fail}\}$$
$$\quad\text{where fail}=\lambda\sigma\,.\,\text{wrong}$$
$$\quad\text{and}\quad \rho'=\langle\rho_1,\kappa\rangle$$
$$\mathbf{E}[\![\varepsilon\ \Omega\ \varepsilon']\!]\rho\kappa=\mathbf{E}[\![\varepsilon]\!]\rho\kappa'$$
$$\quad\text{where }\kappa'=\lambda\text{v},\sigma\,.\,\mathbf{E}[\![\varepsilon']\!]\rho\kappa''\sigma$$
$$\qquad\text{where }\kappa''=\lambda\text{v}',\sigma\,.\,\kappa(\mathbf{O}[\![\Omega]\!]\langle\text{v},\text{v}'\rangle)\sigma$$
$$\mathbf{E}[\![-\varepsilon]\!]\rho\kappa=\mathbf{E}[\![\varepsilon]\!]\rho\{\lambda\text{v},\sigma\,.\,\kappa(-\text{v})\sigma\}$$

The definition of **O** is as before.

The meaning of an integer constant, given an environment, a continuation to use the value and a store, is to apply the continuation to the value of the constant. The meaning of a variable expression, given an environment, a continuation and a store, is to apply the continuation to the value of the variable in the store. The meaning of **valof** γ given an environment and a continuation is the meaning of the command, γ, in an updated environment and a special 'fail' continuation. The updated environment contains the continuation of the **valof** γ for the **resultis** to use. The fail continuation should never be invoked and results in a 'wrong' computation.

$$\mathbf{P}[\![\xi:=\varepsilon]\!]\rho\theta\sigma=\mathbf{E}[\![\varepsilon]\!]\rho\{\lambda\text{v},\sigma'\,.\,\theta(\sigma'[\text{v}/\xi])\}\sigma$$
$$\mathbf{P}[\![\mathbf{if}\ \varepsilon\ \mathbf{then}\ \gamma\ \mathbf{else}\ \gamma']\!]\rho\theta=\mathbf{E}[\![\varepsilon]\!]\rho\{\text{Cond}(\mathbf{P}[\![\gamma]\!]\rho\theta,\mathbf{P}[\![\gamma']\!]\rho\theta)\}$$
$$\mathbf{P}[\![\mathbf{while}\ \varepsilon\ \mathbf{do}\ \gamma]\!]\rho\theta=\mathbf{E}[\![\varepsilon]\!]\rho\ \{\text{Cond}(\mathbf{P}[\![\gamma]\!]\rho\{\mathbf{P}[\![\mathbf{while}\ \varepsilon\ \mathbf{do}\ \gamma]\!]\rho\theta\},\theta)\}$$
$$\mathbf{P}[\![\mathbf{skip}]\!]\rho\theta=\theta$$
$$\mathbf{P}[\![\gamma;\gamma']\!]\rho\theta=\mathbf{P}[\![\gamma]\!]\rho\{\mathbf{P}[\![\gamma']\!]\rho\theta\}$$
$$\mathbf{P}[\![\mathbf{begin}\ \phi_i:\gamma_i\ \mathbf{end}]\!]\rho\theta=\theta_1$$
$$\quad\text{where }\theta_i=\mathbf{P}[\![\gamma_i]\!]\rho'\theta_{i+1},\ \forall i=1\,..\,n;\ \theta_{n+1}=\theta$$
$$\quad\text{and}\quad\rho'=\langle\rho_1[\theta_i/\phi_i],\rho_2\rangle$$
$$\mathbf{P}[\![\text{write}\ \varepsilon]\!]\rho\theta=\mathbf{E}[\![\varepsilon]\!]\rho\{\lambda\text{v},\sigma\,.\langle\text{v},\theta\sigma\rangle\}$$
$$\mathbf{P}[\![\mathbf{resultis}\ \varepsilon]\!]\rho\theta=\mathbf{E}[\![\varepsilon]\!]\rho\{\rho_2\}$$
$$\mathbf{P}[\![\mathbf{goto}\ \phi]\!]\rho\theta=\rho_1[\![\phi]\!]$$
$$\mathbf{P}[\![\phi:\gamma]\!]=\mathbf{P}[\![\gamma]\!]$$

The meaning of an assignment given an environment, a continuation and a store is to evaluate the expression with the environment, an expression kontinuation which will use the value given to update a store, and the store. The meaning of an **if** command is to evaluate the expression with the given environment and an expression kontinuation which uses the value of the expression to select between the two alternative commands.

The meaning of **resultis** ε is to evaluate ε with the given environment and with a new expression kontinuation which is the second component of the environment. Recall that $\mathbf{E}[\![\mathbf{valof}\ \gamma]\!]$ set that component equal to the expression kontinuation of the **valof** construction. So when a **resultis** is executed within a **valof**, the expression is evaluated and the value is taken to 'the end' of the **valof**. If a **resultis** is executed outside any **valof** then an initial continuation $\{\lambda v, \sigma . \perp\}$ is used and the computation is undefined. Alternatively, if no **resultis** is executed in a **valof** then control drops out to the 'fail' continuation and gives a 'wrong' answer.

7.4.1 *Examples*

Some examples are given below to increase familiarity with the definitions. To execute the program fragment

x := 1; y := 2

with environment ρ, continuation θ and store σ, one can think of the situation graphically:

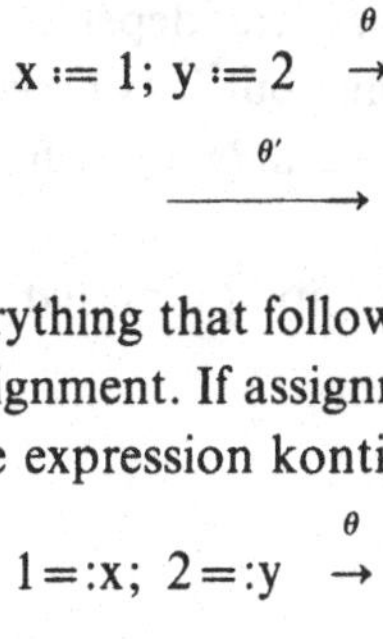

θ is everything that follows the fragment; θ' is everything that follows the first assignment. If assignment were written $\varepsilon =: \xi$ it would be even clearer with the expression kontinuations:

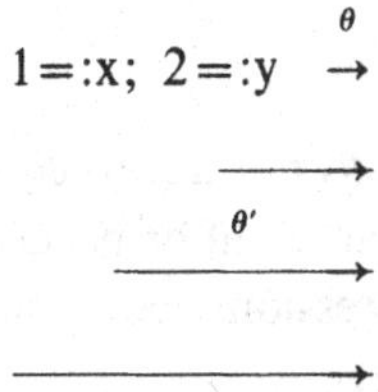

$$\mathbf{P}[\![x := 1;\ y := 2]\!]\rho\theta\sigma = \mathbf{P}[\![x := 1]\!]\rho\{\theta'\}\sigma$$
$$\text{where } \theta' = \mathbf{P}[\![y := 2]\!]\rho\theta$$

It is a useful exercise to check that types really match.

$$\mathbf{P}\text{: } \mathbf{Cmd} \to \mathbf{Env} \to \mathbf{Cont} \to \mathbf{S} \to \mathbf{Ans}$$
$$\mathbf{P}[\![y := 2]\!]\text{: } \mathbf{Env} \to \mathbf{Cont} \to \mathbf{S} \to \mathbf{Ans}$$
$$\mathbf{P}[\![y := 2]\!]\rho\text{: } \mathbf{Cont} \to \mathbf{S} \to \mathbf{Ans}$$
$$\mathbf{P}[\![y := 2]\!]\rho\theta\text{: } \mathbf{S} \to \mathbf{Ans} = \mathbf{Cont}$$

As an example containing a jump out of an expression:

x := **valof begin goto** 99; **resultis** 7 **end**; 99: **skip**

If this is executed with environment ρ, continuation θ and store σ, then $\rho_1[\![\phi]\!]=\theta$.

$$\begin{aligned}
&\mathbf{P}[\![\mathrm{x} := \ldots]\!]\rho\theta\sigma\\
&=\mathbf{E}[\![\mathbf{valof}\ldots]\!]\rho\kappa\sigma\\
&=\mathbf{P}[\![\mathbf{begin}\ldots\mathbf{end}]\!]\rho'\{\mathrm{fail}\}\sigma\\
&=\mathbf{P}[\![\mathbf{goto}\ 99]\!]\rho'\{\mathbf{P}[\![\mathbf{resultis}\ 7]\!]\rho'\{\mathrm{fail}\}\sigma\\
&=\rho_1'[\![99]\!]\sigma\\
&=\mathbf{P}[\![\mathbf{skip}]\!]\rho\theta\sigma\\
&=\theta\ \sigma\\
&\quad\text{where } \rho'=\langle\rho_1,\kappa\rangle\\
&\quad\text{and}\quad \kappa=\{\lambda \mathrm{v},\sigma'.\theta(\sigma'[\mathrm{v}/\mathrm{x}])\}
\end{aligned}$$

The assignment to x is never carried out.

7.5 Declaration continuations

If declarations (see §6.3) can contain expressions and if there may be side-effects and sequencers in expressions then a declaration can be jumped out of. Exactly what the consequences are depends on the semantics of the particular programming language but it is necessary to introduce *declaration continuations*, **Dcont**, to be able to define those semantics.

There may be syntactic restrictions on the jumps permitted in such circumstances. For example, given

$\phi_1 : \gamma_1$;
begin const $\xi =$ **valof** γ_2; $\phi_2 : \gamma_3$ **end**;
$\phi_3 : \gamma_4$

It could be usual to allow γ_2 to jump to ϕ_1 or to ϕ_3 but not to ϕ_2 because this would avoid completing the declaration which might be needed by γ_3.

To define sequencers in a language with expressions, commands and declarations requires three sorts of continuation:

θ: $\mathbf{Cont}=\mathbf{S}\rightarrow\mathbf{Ans}$
κ: $\mathbf{Kont}=\mathbf{Ev}\rightarrow\mathbf{S}\rightarrow\mathbf{Ans}$
χ: $\mathbf{Dcont}=\mathbf{Env}\rightarrow\mathbf{S}\rightarrow\mathbf{Ans}$

Just as an expression kontinuation uses a value to produce a computation (continuation), so a declaration continuation uses an environment to produce a computation.

The valuation functions for expressions, commands and declarations have types:

$$\mathbf{E, L, R: Exp \to Env \to Kont \to S \to Ans}$$
$$\mathbf{P: Cmd \to Env \to Cont \to S \to Ans}$$
$$\mathbf{D: Dec \to Env \to Dcont \to S \to Ans}$$

The environment must contain at least a component for mapping identifiers onto denotable values:

$$\rho\text{: } \mathbf{Env = Ide \to Dv}$$
$$\mathbf{S = Int \times Store}$$
$$\sigma\text{: } \mathbf{Store = Locn \to Sv}$$

If identifiers can stand for variables, procedures and labels, as in Algol-68, then at least the following is needed:

$$\mathbf{Dv = Locn + Proc + Cont}$$
$$\mathbf{Proc = Cont \to S \to Ans}$$

A **Proc** requires a **Cont** as parameter, as return address, before it can produce a computation. A label denotes a continuation as before.

The equations for declarations become:

Dec:

$\delta ::= \mathbf{var}\ \xi \mid \mathbf{const}\ \xi = \varepsilon \mid$
$\quad \mathbf{proc}\ \xi = \gamma \mid \delta; \delta$

$$\mathbf{D}[\![\mathbf{var}\ \xi]\!]\rho\chi\langle \mathrm{f}, \sigma\rangle = \chi\ \rho[\mathrm{f}/\xi]\ \langle \mathrm{f}+1, \sigma\rangle$$
$$\mathbf{D}[\![\mathbf{const}\ \xi = \varepsilon]\!]\rho\chi\langle \mathrm{f}, \sigma\rangle = \mathbf{R}[\![\varepsilon]\!]\rho\kappa\langle \mathrm{f}, \sigma\rangle$$
$$\text{where } \kappa = \{\lambda \mathrm{v}, \langle \mathrm{f}', \sigma'\rangle .\ \chi\ \rho[\mathrm{v}/\xi]\ \langle \mathrm{f}', \sigma'\rangle\}$$
$$\mathbf{D}[\![\mathbf{proc}\ \xi = \gamma]\!]\rho\chi\langle \mathrm{f}, \sigma\rangle = \chi\ \rho'\ \langle \mathrm{f}, \sigma\rangle$$
$$\text{where } \rho' = \rho[\mathrm{p}/\xi]$$
$$\text{where } \mathrm{p} = \lambda\theta, \langle \mathrm{f}, \sigma\rangle .\ \mathbf{P}[\![\gamma]\!]\rho'\theta\langle \mathrm{f}, \sigma\rangle$$
$$\mathbf{D}[\![\delta; \delta']\!]\rho\chi\langle \mathrm{f}, \sigma\rangle = \mathbf{D}[\![\delta]\!]\rho\chi'\langle \mathrm{f}, \sigma\rangle$$
$$\text{where } \chi' = \lambda\rho', \langle \mathrm{f}', \sigma'\rangle .\ \mathbf{D}[\![\delta']\!]\rho'\chi\langle \mathrm{f}', \sigma'\rangle$$

The meaning of **var** ξ, given an environment, a declaration continuation and a state, is to apply the continuation to a new environment and a new state. The new environment binds ξ to the first free location in the old state. The new state is the old state with the free-space counter advanced by one. In other words, reserve a location and bind it to ξ.

To execute **const** $\xi = \varepsilon$ in an environment, a declaration continuation and a state, evaluate the expression in the environment, a new expression kontinuation, and the state. The expression kontinuation binds the value to ξ, producing an updated environment which is given to the declaration continuation. If the expression causes a jump to be executed then the continuation can be discarded and the declaration is abandoned.

The rule for a sequence of declarations specifies that the first declaration is executed with a continuation which executes the rest of the sequence and then the rest of the program. This means that

const n = 10; **const** nplus1 = n + 1; ...

causes 10 to be bound to n and 11 to be bound to nplus1. In some programming languages a group of declarations are performed in 'parallel' as in

Dec:
$\delta ::= \textbf{const}\ \xi^{+} = \varepsilon^{+} \mid \ldots$

Given

$\textbf{const}\ \xi_1 = \varepsilon_1,\ \xi_2 = \varepsilon_2$

the result is

$$\lambda\rho, \chi, \langle \mathrm{f}, \sigma\rangle . \mathbf{E}[\![\varepsilon_1]\!]\rho\kappa'\langle \mathrm{f}, \sigma\rangle$$
$$\text{where } \kappa' = \lambda \mathrm{v}, \langle \mathrm{f}', \sigma'\rangle . \mathbf{D}[\![\textbf{const}\ \xi_2 = \varepsilon_2]\!]\rho\chi''\langle \mathrm{f}', \sigma'\rangle$$
$$\text{where } \chi'' = \lambda\rho' . \chi\ \rho'[\mathrm{v}/\xi_1]$$

so that if ξ_1 appears in ε_2 it is undefined there so ξ_2 should not be defined.

We have already seen the definition of named, parameterless procedures and the implicit declaration of labels as in

$\gamma ::= \textbf{begin}\ \phi_i : \gamma_i\ \textbf{end} \mid \ldots$

If a label, ϕ, is an ordinary identifier as in Algol, it is necessary to check that it does stand for a label value:

$$\mathbf{P}[\![\textbf{goto}\ \phi]\!]\rho\theta\langle \mathrm{f}, \sigma\rangle = \text{if } \mathbf{isCont}(\rho[\![\phi]\!]) \text{ then } \rho[\![\phi]\!]\langle \mathrm{f}, \sigma\rangle \text{ else wrong}$$

If labels have a distinctive syntax, as in Pascal where they are decimal numerals, then either they can be treated as identifiers that happen to consist entirely of digits or the environment can be redefined:

$$\mathbf{Env} = (\mathbf{Ide} \to \mathbf{Dv}) \times (\mathbf{Labels} \to \mathbf{Cont})$$
$$\mathbf{Dv} = \mathbf{Locn} + \mathbf{Proc} + \mathbf{Int}$$

The clauses that look up identifiers and labels in the environment must be changed to select the appropriate component.

7.6 Functions and parameters

Functions produce a result and require an expression kontinuation as the return address to use that value:

$$\mathbf{Func} = \mathbf{Kont} \to \mathbf{S} \to \mathbf{Ans}$$

Parameter passing can be derived from the definition in direct semantics (§6.3.5) and declarations above (§7.5).

$$\mathbf{Procl} = \mathbf{Ev} \to \mathbf{Proc}$$

$$\mathbf{P}[\![\xi(\varepsilon)]\!]\rho\theta\langle f, \sigma\rangle = \text{if } \mathbf{isProcl}(p) \text{ then } \mathbf{E}[\![\varepsilon]\!]\rho\kappa\langle f, \sigma\rangle \text{ else wrong}$$
$$\text{where } p = \rho[\![\xi]\!]$$
$$\text{and } \kappa = \lambda v, \langle f, \sigma\rangle . p\ v\ \theta\ \langle f, \sigma\rangle$$

For example, by-value parameter passing can be defined by:

$$\mathbf{D}[\![\mathbf{proc}\ \xi(\xi') = \gamma]\!]\rho\chi\langle f, \sigma\rangle = \chi\rho'\langle f, \sigma\rangle$$
$$\text{where } \rho' = \rho[p/\xi]$$
$$\text{and } p = \lambda v, \theta, \langle f, \sigma\rangle . \mathbf{P}[\![\gamma]\!]\ \rho'[v/\xi']\ \theta\ \langle f, \sigma\rangle$$
$$\text{where deref} = \lambda v . \text{if } \mathbf{isLocn}(v) \text{ then } \sigma v \text{ else } v$$
$$\text{and } v' = \text{deref } v$$

The formal parameter ξ' is bound to the value of the actual parameter.

7.7 Standard semantics

All of the threads of this chapter can now be pulled together into what is known as *standard semantics*. Semantics in this style are sufficient for describing the features of most sequential programming languages and hence for comparing them formally. This is a very useful property although the fit with a particular programming language may not be quite optimal.

$$\mathbf{Ev} = \mathbf{Int} + \mathbf{Locn} + \ldots$$
$$\mathbf{Dv} = \mathbf{Int} + \mathbf{Locn} + \mathbf{Proc} + \ldots$$
$$\mathbf{Sv} = \mathbf{Int} + \ldots$$
$$\mathbf{Bv} = \mathbf{Int} + \ldots$$
$$\mathbf{Ans} = \{\text{wrong}, \text{finish}\} + \mathbf{Bv} \times \mathbf{Ans}$$
$$\theta: \mathbf{Cont} = \mathbf{S} \to \mathbf{Ans}$$
$$\kappa: \mathbf{Kont} = \mathbf{Ev} \to \mathbf{S} \to \mathbf{Ans}$$
$$\chi: \mathbf{Dcont} = \mathbf{Env} \to \mathbf{S} \to \mathbf{Ans}$$
$$\sigma: \mathbf{Store} = \mathbf{Locn} \to \mathbf{Sv}$$
$$\rho: \mathbf{Env} = \mathbf{Ide} \to \mathbf{Dv} \times \mathbf{Kont}$$
$$\mathbf{S} = \mathbf{Int} \times \mathbf{Store}$$
$$\mathbf{E}, \mathbf{L}, \mathbf{R}: \mathbf{Exp} \to \mathbf{Env} \to \mathbf{Kont} \to \mathbf{S} \to \mathbf{Ans}$$
$$\mathbf{P}: \mathbf{Cmd} \to \mathbf{Env} \to \mathbf{Cont} \to \mathbf{S} \to \mathbf{Ans}$$
$$\mathbf{D}: \mathbf{Dec} \to \mathbf{Env} \to \mathbf{Dcont} \to \mathbf{S} \to \mathbf{Ans}$$

The exact definitions of **E**, **P**, **D** and so on depend on the programming language under study, but representative examples based on this chapter are given below. **E** is largely as defined before:

$$\mathbf{E}[\![\xi]\!]\rho\kappa\langle \mathrm{f},\sigma\rangle = \text{if } \mathbf{isEv}(\mathrm{v}) \text{ then } \kappa\mathrm{v}\langle \mathrm{f},\sigma\rangle \text{ else wrong}$$
$$\text{where } \mathrm{v} = \rho_1[\![\xi]\!]$$
$$\mathbf{E}[\![\mathbf{valof}\ \gamma]\!]\rho\kappa\langle \mathrm{f},\sigma\rangle = \mathbf{P}[\![\gamma]\!]\rho'\{\mathrm{fail}\}\langle \mathrm{f},\sigma\rangle$$
$$\text{where fail} = \lambda\langle \mathrm{f},\sigma\rangle.\ \text{wrong}$$
$$\text{and} \quad \rho' = \langle \rho_1, \kappa\rangle$$

The other clauses for **E** are as in §7.4. To cover left and right values **L** and **R** are used:

$$\mathbf{L}[\![\xi]\!]\rho\kappa\langle \mathrm{f},\sigma\rangle = \mathbf{E}[\![\varepsilon]\!]\rho\{\mathrm{check}\}\langle \mathrm{f},\sigma\rangle$$
$$\text{where check} = \lambda\mathrm{v}, \langle \mathrm{f},\sigma\rangle.\ \text{if } \mathbf{isLocn}(\mathrm{v}) \text{ then } \kappa\mathrm{v}\langle \mathrm{f},\sigma\rangle \text{ else wrong}$$
$$\mathbf{R}[\![\varepsilon]\!]\rho\kappa\langle \mathrm{f},\sigma\rangle = \mathbf{E}[\![\varepsilon]\!]\rho\{\mathrm{deref}\}\langle \mathrm{f},\sigma\rangle$$
$$\text{where deref} = \lambda\mathrm{v}, \langle \mathrm{f},\sigma\rangle.\ \text{if } \mathbf{isLocn}(\mathrm{v}) \text{ then } \kappa(\sigma\mathrm{v})\langle \mathrm{f},\sigma\rangle \text{ else } \kappa\mathrm{v}\langle \mathrm{f},\sigma\rangle$$

The definitions for **D** are as in §7.5. The clauses of **P** for assignment, procedure call and **goto** are:

$$\mathbf{P}[\![\varepsilon := \varepsilon']\!]\rho\theta\langle \mathrm{f},\sigma\rangle = \mathbf{L}[\![\varepsilon]\!]\rho\theta'\langle \mathrm{f},\sigma\rangle$$
$$\text{where } \theta' = \lambda\langle \mathrm{f},\sigma\rangle.\ \mathbf{R}[\![\varepsilon']\!]\rho\theta''\langle \mathrm{f},\sigma\rangle$$
$$\text{where } \theta'' = \lambda\mathrm{v}, \langle \mathrm{f},\sigma\rangle.\ \theta\langle \mathrm{f},\sigma[\mathrm{v}/\mathrm{l}]\rangle$$
$$\mathbf{P}[\![\xi]\!]\rho\theta\langle \mathrm{f},\sigma\rangle = \text{if } \mathbf{isProc}(\mathrm{v}) \text{ then } \mathrm{v}\theta\langle \mathrm{f},\sigma\rangle \text{ else wrong}$$
$$\text{where } \mathrm{v} = \rho_1[\![\xi]\!]$$
$$\mathbf{P}[\![\mathbf{goto}\ \phi]\!]\rho\theta\langle \mathrm{f},\sigma\rangle = \text{if } \mathbf{isCont}(\mathrm{v}) \text{ then } \mathrm{v}\langle \mathrm{f},\sigma\rangle \text{ else wrong}$$
$$\text{where } \mathrm{v} = \rho_1[\![\xi]\!]$$
$$\mathbf{P}[\![\mathbf{resultis}\ \varepsilon]\!]\rho\theta\langle \mathrm{f},\sigma\rangle = \mathbf{E}[\![\varepsilon]\!]\rho\rho_2\langle \mathrm{f},\sigma\rangle$$

7.8 An Algol-68 translation

It is not practical to translate the semantics discussed above into standard Pascal. **function** and **procedure** stand apart from other types in Pascal and cannot be given symbolic names. This means that the function headings in any such translation grow large. However, it can be translated easily into standard Algol-68;† Pagan [47] suggests the use of Algol-68 extended with partial parameterization.

A simple parser can be written to return a tree data structure and, as pointed out by Pagan, it is convenient to make use of the Algol-68 **union mode** to stand for alternation, '|', in the syntax. The 'uniting' coercion of Algol-68 also enables many injections into **unions** to be implicit.

† In Algol-68, types are called **modes**.

```
mode assign = struct(exp lhs, rhs),
     semi = struct(cmd left, right),
     ifstat = struct(exp b, cmd gtrue, gfalse),
     whiles = struct(exp b, cmd g),
     block = struct(dec d, cmd g),
     labcmd = struct(label 1, cmd g),
     g0t0 = label,
     oneexp = struct(int tag, exp e); c write ε or resultis ε c
mode label = int;
mode cmdnode = union(assign, semi, ifstat,
                     whiles, block, alfa c call c,
                     labcmd, g0t0, oneexp);
mode cmd = ref cmdnode;
mode bexp = struct(opr opr, exp left, right),
     uexp = struct(opr opr, exp son),
     var = alfa;
mode expnode = union(bexp, uexp, var, int, cvalofc cmd);
mode exp = ref expnode;
mode vardec = alfa,
     constdec = struct(alfa id, exp e),
     procdec = struct(alfa id, cmd g),
     declist = struct(dec left, right);
mode decnode = union(vardec, constdec, procdec, declist);
mode dec = ref decnode;
```

As there is no enumerated type in Algol-68, operators (**mode opr**) can be represented by small integers.

The semantic domains are also coded as **modes**:

```
mode ev = union(int, locn),      c = Int + Locn c
     sv = int,
     cont = proc(int, store)ans,
     kont = proc(ev, int, store)ans,
     dcont = proc(env, int, store)ans;
```

We would like to define

```
mode aproc = proc(cont, int, store)ans,
     dv = union(int, locn, cont, aproc) c for const, var, label, proc c
     env = struct(proc(alfa)dv rho1, kont rho2);
```

Unfortunately the scope rules of stack-based languages such as Algol-68 prevent rho1 from returning an **aproc** as an instance of a **dv**; the **aproc** would depend on local objects of rho1. Fortunately, it is possible to split the environment into components for constants and variables, labels, procedures and the **valof–resultis** kontinuation.

```
mode vnv = proc(alfa)dv,
     lnv = proc(label, int, store)ans,
     pnv = proc(alfa, cont, int, store)ans;
mode dv = union(int, locn);
mode env = struct(vnv vnv, pnv pnv, lnv lnv, kont kont);
```

This leaves the question of whether a name can stand for a variable and a procedure simultaneously to syntax.

Ideally **mode locn = int**, but then **dv = union(int, locn)** is illegal because **locn** is coercible to, in fact identical to, **int**. One fiddle around this is

```
mode locn = struct(int l, dont care);
```

Answers, **Ans**, are programmed as:

```
mode ans = union(alfa c wrong or finish c, ref anscell);
mode anscell = struct(bv v, ans next);
```

The interpreter must also contain simple list-processing routines to construct answers and to print them out. Note that because Algol-68 does not use lazy evaluation, the interpreter does not define programs that do not terminate. This could be programmed around by leaving the answer in an Algol-68 output file.

It is convenient to define

```
proc wrong = (string s)ans:
   (print( s ); ans( "wrong      " ) );
```

so that where 'wrong' appears in the formal semantics, the interpreter can call **proc** wrong with an informative message.

The main interpreter routines are **E**, **L**, **R**, **D** and **P**.

```
proc E = (exp ex, env e, kont k, int f, store s)ans:
case ex in
(var v):  k( (vnv of e)(v), f, s),
(int n):  k( n, f, s),
(cmd g): (c valof γ c
             cont fail = (int f, store s)ans:
                wrong(" fail: fell out of valof");
             env new e = (vnv of e, pnv of e, lnv of e, k);
             P(g, new e, fail, f, s)
         ),
...
esac;
```

L produces left values or locations and **R** produces storable values.

```
proc L=(exp ex, env e, kont k, int f, store s)ans:
  (kont check=(ev v, int f, store s)ans:
     case v in
      (locn l): k(l, f, s)
      out wrong(" not left value")
      esac
    E(ex, e, check, f, s)
  );
proc R=(exp ex, env e, kont k, int f, store s)ans:
  (kont deref=(ev v, int f, store s)ans:
      case v in
      (int i): k(i, f, s),
      (locn l): k(s(l), f, s)
      esac;
    E(ex, e, deref, f, s)
  );
```

Declarations are processed by **proc D**:

```
proc D=(dec d, env e, dcont dc, int f, store s) ans:
  if d is nil
    then dc(e, f, s)
    else case d in
         (vardec vd): (vnv new vnv=(alfa id)dv:
                          if id=vd then locn(f,0)
                          else (vnv of e)(id) fi;
                      env new e=(new vnv, pnv of e, lnv of e, kont of e);
                      dc(new e, f+1, s)
                      ),
         ...
         esac
  fi;
```

Finally, **proc P** defines commands:

```
proc P=(cmd g, env e, cont t, int f, store s)ans:
  if g is nil
    then c skip c t(f, s)
    else case g in
         (semi g1g2): (cont g2=(int f, store s)ans:
                           P(right of g1g2, e, t, f, s);
                       P(left of g1g2, g2, e, f, s)
                      ),
```

```
        (ifstat if):   (kont cond=(ev b, int f, store s) ans:
                          case b in
                          (int i): P(if i=1
                                        then gtrue of if
                                        else gfalse of if
                                     fi,
                                     e, t, f, s)
                          out wrong(" bad switch")
                          esac;
                        R(b of if, e, cond, f, s)
                       ),
        ...
        (alfa procid): (pnv of e)(procid, t, f, s),
        (g0t0 n): (lnv of e)(n, f, s),
        ...
        esac
   fi;
```

To parse and execute a program:

show(**P**(parser, start env, finish, 0, empty store))

7.9 Exercises

1. Show in some detail how the semantic equations define the execution of the following program:

   begin n := 3; f := 1;
   99: f := f∗n; n := n − 1;
   if n > 1 **then goto** 99 **else skip**;
   write f
   end

2. Compare the semantics of

   Exp:
   ε ::= **begin** γ; ε **end**

   with the semantics of

   Exp: ε ::= **valof** γ **Cmd:** γ ::= **resultis** ε

   Does this suggest that one is 'better' than the other?

3. Give semantic equations for **break** and **continue**. These may only be executed without error when *textually* within a loop. The effect of **break** is to terminate the closest enclosing loop altogether. A **continue** causes the current iteration, only, to be terminated and control passes back to the loop test.

4. Define **return** for procedures and **return** ε for functions.
5. Add input to the standard semantics of this chapter.

   Exp:
   ε ::= read | . . .
6. Define the semantics of a conditional expression:

   Exp:
   ε ::= **if** ε **then** ε **else** ε | . . .
7. **Project:** implement continuation semantics in a suitable programming language such as Algol-68 or ML or, given such an interpreter, modify it to include the solutions to questions 3 to 6.

8
Data structures and data types

There is great variety amongst programming languages in the area of data structures and type checking. It is only possible to deal with some of the more straightforward issues in this chapter.

Some languages, such as BCPL [52], are typeless, or have only one type. All BCPL variables have the type 'word'. This enables BCPL to rival assembly code in application while being much more readable and concise. There are dangers, however; the compiler cannot detect type errors because there are none.

Languages that do provide types are characterized by the kind of data structures, the time at which types are checked and how much the programmer can define. Simple types, such as integer, stand for basic domains like **Int**. Structured types – arrays and records – stand for derived domains. There are hard problems, however, in deciding what a programmer-defined type, particularly one defined by possibly recursive equations, stands for – see recent conference proceedings [1, 2, 31]. This is obviously connected with recursive domains (§4.3).

APL [27] is a *dynamically typed* language. Each constant has a particular type – integer, character or vector or array of one of these. The value currently assigned to a variable therefore has some type, but both the value *and* the type may change as the program runs. Each APL operator is only applicable to certain types, so it is possible to add 1 to an integer or to a vector of integers but not to a character. Operators must be interpreted and type checking is done as the program runs and can be included in the (dynamic) semantics of the language.

In fact at least two types, integer constants or **int** and integer variables or **ref int** in Algol-68 terms, have already crept into the semantics of previous chapters. An **int** cannot be assigned to and this was checked for in the semantics (§6.3.2, §7.7). Procedures are a further type.

The Algol family of languages, including Algol-60, Algol-68, Pascal and Ada, are *statically typed*. The types of all constants and named objects in a program can be evaluated without running the program and any misuse of an object can be detected by a compiler. The type information allows efficient machine code to be generated. It also allows operators to be *overloaded* so that '+' can stand for integer and real addition, set union and even string concatenation. Within this family of languages there are subtle differences such as whether two different but structurally equivalent types are considered to be the same or not.

Static type checking is variously labelled as part of syntax, as part of semantics or as static semantics. It can in fact be defined by attribute grammars. It can be specified within the usual (dynamic) semantics of the language as a special case in which types happen not to change. It can also be specified by a separate set of semantic rules. The last is closest to the spirit of static type checking. There is a very strong practical constraint on type checking: there should be a decision procedure for it. A programmer is prepared, perhaps resigned, to see some programs loop but not to see the compiler do so. In addition, type checking should not take much more than linear time in terms of program length. In return for more expressive power, some might accept a relaxation of this to a semi-decision-procedure where the checking would terminate on a correctly typed program but might loop on an incorrect one. Coppo [10] has suggested polymorphic type mechanisms in this class.

Dynamic types can be added to the semantics already given by suitable additions to various domains and to the set of operators. The following sections examine aspects of data structures and static type checking. It is only possible to cover common core ideas from the spectrum of types.

8.1 Dynamic semantics of data structures

A simple set of data-types (suitable for static checking) and operations on them might have the syntax:

Dec:
$\delta ::=$ **var** $\xi : \tau \mid \ldots$

Texp:
$\tau ::=$ **int** $\mid$ **bool** $\mid \ldots$
  array $[\nu : \nu]$ **of** $\tau \mid$
  record $\xi^* : \tau^*$ **end**

Exp:
$\varepsilon ::= \nu \mid$ **true** $\mid$ **false** $\mid$
  $\varepsilon[\varepsilon] \mid \varepsilon . \xi \mid \ldots$

Texp stands for type expression.

For inclusion in the usual dynamic semantics, this calls for an expansion of denotable and expressible values.

Dv = **Locn** + **Array** + **Record** + ...
Ev = **Int** + **Bool** + **Locn** + **Array** + **Record** + ...

An environment, ρ: **Env** = **Ide** → **Dv**, maps a named object onto whatever it has been declared to be.

An array can be modelled by a function from subscript values to locations:

Array = **Int** → **Locn**

Each array is a finite function, so a multiple of locations would also do. If the subscript is out of range then $\perp$ or 'wrong' can be specified. If other basic types can be used as subscripts, then

Type:
τ ::= **array** [ε:ε] **of** τ | ...
Array = **Bv** → **Locn**

Greater generality, such as array constants, can be allowed by

Array = **Bv** → **Dv**

A record maps field selectors onto locations:

Record = **Ide** → **Locn**

This bears a striking similarity to **Env** = **Ide** → **Dv** and if record constants containing arbitrary denotable values are allowed,

Record = **Env**

makes sense. This leads to a neat semantics for a Pascal style **with** statement – see Gordon [21]. Like an array, a record is a finite function.

8.2 Static type checking

It is possible to give a denotational semantics of a language that defines type checking rather than its usual execution. This is an example of a non-standard interpretation of a programming language. The semantic domains are somewhat different:

Type = {**Int**, **Bool**} ∪ {**Array**(t, t′) | t, t′: **Type**} ∪ {**Record**(ξ*, t*)}
 ∪ {**Ref** t | t: **Type**} ∪ {wrong}
Env = **Ide** → **Type**

In this section, **Int** should be strictly taken to be the name of the abstract domain of integers, not the domain itself, to avoid difficult questions.

There are no programmer-named types, yet, and an environment maps constants and variables onto their types.

$$\begin{aligned}
&\mathbf{T}: \mathbf{Texp} \to \mathbf{Type}\\
&\mathbf{D}: \mathbf{Dec} \to \mathbf{Env} \to (\mathbf{Env} \cup \{\text{wrong}\})\\
&\mathbf{E}: \mathbf{Exp} \to \mathbf{Env} \to \mathbf{Type}\\
&\mathbf{C}: \mathbf{Cmd} \to \mathbf{Env} \to \{\text{ok, wrong}\}\\
&\mathbf{O}: \mathbf{Opr} \to \mathbf{Type}^2 \to \mathbf{Type}
\end{aligned}$$

$$\begin{aligned}
&\mathbf{T}[\![\mathbf{int}]\!] = \mathbf{Int}\\
&\mathbf{T}[\![\mathbf{bool}]\!] = \mathbf{Bool}\\
&\mathbf{T}[\![\varepsilon : \varepsilon']\!]\rho = \text{if } t \in \{\mathbf{Int}, \mathbf{Bool}\} \text{ and } t = t' \text{ then } t \text{ else wrong}\\
&\quad \text{where } t = \text{deref}(\mathbf{E}[\![\varepsilon]\!]\rho)\\
&\quad \text{and } \ t' = \text{deref}(\mathbf{E}[\![\varepsilon']\!]\rho)
\end{aligned}$$

$$\begin{aligned}
&\text{deref}(\mathbf{Ref}\ t) = t\\
&\text{deref } t = t \qquad \text{otherwise}
\end{aligned}$$

$$\begin{aligned}
&\mathbf{T}[\![\mathbf{array}[\varepsilon : \varepsilon']\mathbf{of}\ \tau]\!]\rho = \text{if } t = \text{wrong or } t' = \text{wrong}\\
&\qquad\qquad\qquad\qquad\qquad \text{then wrong}\\
&\qquad\qquad\qquad\qquad\qquad \text{else } \mathbf{Array}(t, t')\\
&\quad \text{where } t = \mathbf{T}[\![\varepsilon : \varepsilon']\!]\rho\\
&\quad \text{and } \ t' = \mathbf{T}[\![\tau]\!]\rho\\
&\mathbf{T}[\![\mathbf{record}\ \xi^* : \tau^*\ \mathbf{end}]\!]\rho = \text{if wrong} \in \{t^*\} \text{ then wrong else } \mathbf{Record}(\xi^*, t^*)\\
&\quad \text{where } t^* = \mathbf{T}[\![\tau^*]\!]\rho
\end{aligned}$$

$$\begin{aligned}
&\mathbf{E}[\![\nu]\!]\rho = \mathbf{Int}\\
&\mathbf{E}[\![\mathbf{true}]\!]\rho = \mathbf{Bool}\\
&\mathbf{E}[\![\mathbf{false}]\!]\rho = \mathbf{Bool}\\
&\mathbf{E}[\![\xi]\!]\rho = \rho[\![\xi]\!]\\
&\mathbf{E}[\![\varepsilon[\varepsilon']]\!]\rho = \text{if } t = \mathbf{Ref}\ \mathbf{Array}(t_1, t_2) \text{ and } t' = t_1\\
&\qquad\qquad\qquad \text{then } \mathbf{Ref}\ t_2\\
&\qquad\qquad\qquad \text{else wrong}\\
&\text{where } t = \mathbf{E}[\![\varepsilon]\!]\rho\\
&\text{and } \ t' = \text{deref}(\mathbf{E}[\![\varepsilon']\!]\rho)
\end{aligned}$$

Note, the last rule only checks the types in array subscripting; the bound checking must be left to dynamic semantics in general.

$$\begin{aligned}
&\mathbf{E}[\![\varepsilon . \xi]\!] = \text{if } \mathbf{E}[\![\varepsilon]\!]\rho = \mathbf{Ref}\ \mathbf{Record}(\xi^*, t^*) \text{ and } \xi = \xi^*[i]\\
&\qquad\qquad \text{then } \mathbf{Ref}\ t^*[i]\\
&\qquad\qquad \text{else wrong}\\
&\mathbf{E}[\![\varepsilon\Omega\varepsilon]\!]\rho = \mathbf{O}[\![\Omega]\!]\langle \mathbf{E}[\![\varepsilon]\!]\rho, \mathbf{E}[\![\varepsilon']\!]\rho\rangle\\
&\mathbf{O}[\![+]\!]\langle t, t'\rangle = \text{if deref } t = \text{deref } t' = \mathbf{Int} \text{ then } \mathbf{Int} \text{ else wrong}\\
&\quad \text{etc.}
\end{aligned}$$

If preferred, subscripting can be treated as a binary operator and BCPL uses '!' for this purpose. It is not appropriate to treat '.' as an operator and to use $\varepsilon.\varepsilon$ for record selection because the field selector, and so its type, should be calculated statically.

$$\mathbf{D}[\![\mathbf{const}\ \xi=\varepsilon]\!]\rho = \text{ if t=wrong then wrong else } \rho[\text{t}/\xi]$$
$$\text{where t=deref}(\mathbf{E}[\![\varepsilon]\!]\rho)$$

$$\mathbf{D}[\![\mathbf{var}\ \xi:\tau]\!]\rho = \text{if t=wrong then wrong else } \rho[\mathbf{Ref}\ \text{t}/\xi]$$
$$\text{where t} = \mathbf{T}[\![\tau]\!]\rho$$

$$\mathbf{D}[\![\delta;\delta']\!] = \text{if } \mathbf{D}[\![\delta]\!]\rho = \text{wrong then wrong else } \mathbf{D}[\![\delta']\!](\mathbf{D}[\![\delta]\!]\rho)$$

$$\mathbf{C}[\![\gamma;\gamma']\!]\rho = \text{if } \mathbf{C}[\![\gamma]\!]\rho = \text{ok then } \mathbf{C}[\![\gamma']\!]\rho \text{ else wrong}$$

$$\mathbf{C}[\![\mathbf{begin}\ \delta:\gamma\ \mathbf{end}]\!]\rho = \text{if } \mathbf{D}[\![\delta]\!]\rho = \text{wrong then wrong else } \mathbf{C}[\![\gamma]\!](\mathbf{D}[\![\delta]\!]\rho)$$

$$\mathbf{C}[\![\varepsilon:=\varepsilon']\!]\rho = \text{if t} = \mathbf{Ref}\ \text{t}' \text{ then ok else wrong}$$
$$\text{where t} = \mathbf{E}[\![\varepsilon]\!]\rho$$
$$\text{and } \text{t}' = \text{deref}(\mathbf{E}[\![\varepsilon']\!]\rho)$$

$$\mathbf{C}[\![\mathbf{if}\ \varepsilon\ \mathbf{then}\ \gamma\ \mathbf{else}\ \gamma']\!]\rho$$
$$= \text{if b} = \mathbf{Bool} \text{ and r} = \text{r}' = \text{ok then ok else wrong}$$
$$\text{where b} = \text{deref}(\mathbf{E}[\![\varepsilon]\!]\rho)$$
$$\text{and } \langle \text{r}, \text{r}' \rangle = \langle \mathbf{C}[\![\gamma]\!]\rho, \mathbf{C}[\![\gamma']\!]\rho \rangle$$

Other structured commands are checked similarly.

To introduce procedure and function types we can add

$$\mathbf{Type} = \{\mathbf{Proc}(\text{t}^*) \mid \text{t}^* \in \mathbf{Type}^*\} \cup \{\mathbf{Func}(\text{t}^*, \text{t})\} \cup \ldots$$

Depending on the syntax of declarations and commands using these objects, **T**, **E**, **D** and **C** are extended appropriately. Note that programming languages differ greatly on the extent to which procedures and functions are 'first-class objects' capable of assignment and being passed as parameters and results.

8.2.1 *Named types*

Syntactically, named types can be allowed by:

Dec:

$\delta ::= \mathbf{type}\ \xi = \tau \mid \ldots$

A name can then denote a type or a constant or variable of some type.

$$\mathbf{Env} = \mathbf{Ide} \rightarrow \mathbf{Type} + \mathbf{Type}'$$

This reflects the duality between the behaviour of types at compile time and values at run time.

There are now at least two type disciplines possible. Types can be taken as equivalent if they have the same structure or only if they are defined as equal.

type t1 = **array**[1 .. 10]**of int**;
t2, t3 = **array**[1 .. 10]**of int**;

Algol-68 would treat t1, t2 and t3 as equivalent. Some implementations of the original Pascal would do the same and some would only identify t2 and t3.

8.2.2 *Recursive types*

With named types, the possibility of recursive types also appears. Some are clearly reasonable and of course denotational semantics itself depends on recursive domains (§4.3).

type rft = **function**(rft)**int**;
type ftr = **function**(**int**)ftr;
type rat = **array** [1:10] **of** rat

The equivalent of 'rft' and 'ftr' are allowed in Algol-68. Something similar to rft is required for the fixed-point operator, see §3.3.1. Their structures cannot be written out in a finite string of basic types and constructors, but can be represented by finite cyclic graphs, for example:

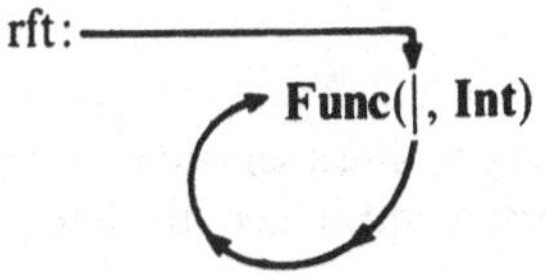

They can also be represented using the fixed-point operator μ (§3.4):

rft = μ 'x. **Func**('x, **Int**)

where 'x is a type variable.

It is possible to write a (terminating) algorithm to compare two such types for equivalence. Type 'rat' and the like are not usually allowed, although the effect can be programmed with the addition of pointers.

8.2.3 *Parameterized types*

It seems a small step to add type parameters to form abstract data-types, for example:

Dec:

type $\xi('\xi^*) = \tau \mid \ldots$

Texp:

$\tau ::= \xi(\tau^+) \mid '\xi \mid \ldots$

This might be used to define lists:

type list('x) = **union(null, record** h:'x; t:list('x) **end)**

In fact this example can be taken as a scheme or shorthand for defining list(**int**), list (**bool**), list(list(**int**)) and so on. MacQueen and Plotkin [33] discuss such types with polymorphism. Note that list is a type constructor or a function on types. This suggests list has the type or *kind* **Type → Type**.

Much harder to deal with are examples like

type nasty('x) = **union(null,**
record h:'x; t:nasty(**record** a:'x; b:'x **end**))

8.3 Non-standard interpretations

A semantics for static type checking resembles a normal dynamic semantics in which all integer values have been collapsed into one representative called **Int**, all booleans collapsed onto **Bool** and so on. The Cousots [11] have shown a whole class of interrelated non-standard semantics or interpretations of a programming language, which are useful for static analysis of programs. Mycroft [42] has used such techniques to identify strict functions in a functional programming language for optimization purposes.

8.4 Exercises

1. Add array declarations and subscripting to direct semantics (Ch 6) and to continuation semantics (Ch 7). **Project:** modify one of the interpreters to include this.
2. Discuss the options in defining the semantics of array operations such as assignment, as in Pascal, and slices and other operators, as in Algol-68.
3. A Pascal enumerated-type declaration, such as

   type colour = (red, green, yellow)

   declares colour to be a certain set of atoms and also declares those atoms to have type colour. How can this be included in static type checking?
4. **Project:** implement the type-checking semantics (§ 8.2) in Pascal or some other suitable programming language.
5. **Project:** for the language of Ch 5, give a non-standard semantics based on the following. A variable's status may be 'set', 'unset' or 'possibly set'. Before a program starts to run every variable is unset. A constant is set. An expression is set if all subexpressions are set. It is unset if any subexpression is unset. Otherwise the expression is possibly set. After an assignment of an expression to a variable, the variable takes the status of the expression. Consider **if** and **while** commands carefully.

   Give a semantics to calculate the status of all variables when a program has stopped. This should only incorporate what can be deduced *statically* without running the program. It must be on the assumption that the program does in fact terminate.

Implement this semantics in a programming language. It could be used to check programs before they are run. Warnings could be printed at the use of unset variables.

9
A Prolog semantics

Ashcroft and Wadge [4] have criticized effort spent on describing existing programming languages and have suggested a more active, prescriptive role for denotational semantics in designing languages of the future. Accepting some truth in this, this chapter contains a semantics for Prolog. While there are existing Prologs, plural, logic programming is still a research area and a denotational semantics is one way to investigate variations in it.

Prolog [9] is a programming language based on first-order predicate logic. A Prolog program can be thought of in two ways. It can be taken to be a set of logical assertions or facts about a world or some part of a world. This is the *declarative semantics* of the program. It can also be taken as a set of procedure definitions which gives its *procedural semantics*.

The declarative semantics are very elegant in that the program stands for some basic facts and certain other facts that logically follow from them. No side-effects or considerations of the order of evaluation are involved. Unfortunately, to make Prolog run and to make it run efficiently, some programs require side-effects such as input–output and the order of evaluation to be taken into account. This can only be understood procedurally.

Here a denotational semantics of a subset of Prolog is given. This defines the backtracking search and unification processes of Prolog. Later the definition is translated into Algol-68 to form an interpreter. Prolog is still a research language and giving a denotational semantics enables it to be compared with other languages in a uniform framework. It is also a basis for investigating the control features of different versions of Prolog, such as the cut and various lazy-evaluation rules [43]. Jones and Mycroft [29] and Nicholson and Foo [45] have given semantics which include cut.

9.1 Prolog

A Prolog program contains *atoms*, *variables*, *functions* and *predicates*. An atom is a constant such as 99 or fred. Variables are written as identifiers starting with a capital letter. Functions appear in conventional prefix notation as in plus(2, 3). Note that Prolog places no interpretation on plus; it does not associate it with any particular arithmetic operator. father(father(john)) may be intended to stand for the paternal grandfather of john, but that is the programmer's interpretation, not Prolog's. A predicate is a truth-valued function such as 'odd' or 'are-married'.

A (basic) *fact* asserts that a predicate applied to some values is true, for example:

```
odd(7).
parents(william, charles, diana).
parents(henry, charles, diana).
parents(charles, philip, elizabeth).
parents(diana, edward, frances).
```

A *rule* may be used to deduce new facts, as in:

```
parent(X, Y) :- parents(X, Y, Z).
```

This can be taken to mean, Y is a parent of X if (:–)there is a Z such that Y and Z are the parents of X. There is another similar rule:

```
parent(X, Y) :- parents(X, Z, Y).
```

Grandparents can be defined by:

```
grandparent(X, G) :- parent(X, P), parent(P, G).
```

G is a grandparent of X if there is a P such that P is a parent of X and G is a parent of P.

The head of a rule, to the left of :–, can also be taken as the name of a procedure. To call grandparent, call parent twice.

This collection of facts and rules might form part of a database. A typical *query* might be

```
?- grandparent(william, philip).
```

This example can be deduced from the database and we would expect the answer 'yes'. Queries can also contain variables and they can be written out:

```
?- grandparent(william, Who), write(Who).
```

This should give the response:

```
philip yes
elizabeth yes
edward yes
frances yes
```

Prolog is a subset of first-order predicate logic called Horn clauses. This allows a reasonably efficient version of a theorem-proving algorithm called *resolution* to form the basis of a Prolog interpreter. Those wishing to discover more about logic and resolution should consult Kowalski [32], Clocksin and Mellish [9] or Nilsson [46]. An informal description of the proof process is given in the next section.

9.1.1 ***Execution***

Given the previous example database and the query

?- grandparent(william, Who), write(Who).

Prolog will attempt to *satisfy* the query by trying to satisfy each predicate in turn. The first predicate

?- grandparent(william, Who).

and the head of the rule

grandparent(X, G) :- parent(X, P), parent(P, G).

have the same predicate name, and can be made identical, or *unified*, by the substitution or unifier [william/X, Who/G]. If this substitution is made in the body of the rule, the result is

?- parent(william, P), parent(P, Who).

What is needed is a parent, P, of william and then a parent of P. parent(william, P) can be unified with the rule head of

parent(X, Y) :- parents(X, Y, Z).

by the unifier [william/X, P/Y]. The body becomes

?- parents(william, P, Z).

This unifies with parents(william, charles, diana) giving [charles/P, diana/Z]. At this stage a parent of william has been found, namely charles, and now it remains to find a parent of charles. The same process will eventually find [philip/Who].

The predicate 'write' always succeeds, and prints its arguments in the output file.

There are two places where an arbitrary choice is made in the search process described. parent(william, P) will unify with either of the two rules defining parent. One choice leads to the father, the other to the mother. This occurs twice giving maternal and paternal grandmothers and grandfathers, so there are four solutions to the query. The declarative semantics specify no preference; the choice is non-deterministic. As Prolog is practised, procedurally, the search is almost invariably sequential. Some interpreters will give one solution with a method for backtracking to find the other solutions; some will give all solutions immediately.

9.1.2 *Example: append*

Lists can be represented by a function, say 'dot'. The empty list is represented by 'nil', and $\langle 1, 2, 3\rangle$ by

```
dot(1, dot(2, dot(3, nil)))
```

A classic Prolog example is a program to join two lists into a third list; it can be expressed as:

```
append(nil, X, X).
append(dot(Head, Tail), List, dot(Head, Rest)) :-
  append(Tail, List, Rest).
```

The result of appending nil and any list X, is X. The result of appending any non-nil list dot(Head, Tail) and any List is dot(Head, Rest) where the result of appending Tail and List is Rest. This is easily seen with the aid of the following diagram:

```
Head . Tail   List
       ___________
Head .    Rest
```

The query

```
?- append(dot(1,dot(2, nil)), dot(3,dot(4, nil)), Z), write(Z).
```

asks Prolog to append $\langle 1,2\rangle$ and $\langle 3,4\rangle$. The query unifies with the rule in the program giving

[1/Head, dot(2, nil)/Tail, dot(3, dot(4, nil))/List,
  dot(Head, Rest)/Z]

This gives the sub-query

```
?- append(dot(2, nil), dot(3, dot(4, nil)), Rest).
```

which also unifies with the rule giving

[2/Head, nil/Tail, dot(3, dot(4, nil))/List,
  dot(Head, Rest')/Rest]

This gives the sub-query

```
?- append(nil, dot(3, dot(4, nil)), Rest').
```

which matches the fact in the program, giving

[dot(3, dot(4, nil))/X, X/Rest']

This is the end of the recursion and it now unwinds giving

[dot(2, dot(3, dot(4, nil)))/Rest]

at the previous level and

[dot(1, dot(2, dot(3, dot(4, nil))))/Z]

at the top level. Lastly, this value for Z is written out.

Real Prolog systems provide a much friendlier syntax including infix operators and a special list notation, so that one can write:

```
?- append([1,2], [3,4], Z), write(Z).
```

However, what is given above is sufficient and close to the internal representations of Prolog.

A very interesting feature of the append program is that it will run backwards!

```
?- append(X, Y, dot(1,dot(2,nil))), write(X), write(Y).
```

will yield two lists which append to form dot(1, dot(2, nil)). The result is

```
nil  dot(1,dot(2,nil))  yes
dot(1,nil)  dot(2,nil)  yes
dot(1,dot(2,nil))  nil  yes
```

There are three solutions.

9.1.3 *Differentiator*

The rules for symbolic differentiation can be written directly in Prolog.

```
d(plus(A, B), X, plus(DA, DB)) :- d(A, X, DA), d(B, X, DB).
d(mult(A, B), X, plus(mult(A, DB), mult(DA, B))) :- d(A, X, DA),
                                                     d(B, X, DB).
d(X, X, 1).
d(Y, X, 0).
```

The differential of A + B with respect to X is DA + DB where the differential of A is DA and the differential of B is DB. The other rules can be read similarly. The query

```
?-d(plus(mult(x, 4), 3), x, Z), write(Z).
```

will give the solutions

```
plus(plus(mult(x, 0), mult(1, 4)), 0)  yes
plus(plus(mult(x, 0), mult(0, 4)), 0)  yes
plus(0, 0)  yes
0  yes
```

The first is correct, if long-winded, (d/dx)(x * 4 + 3) = x * 0 + 1 * 4 + 0 = 4. The last three are incorrect and are caused by the final clause in the program, d(Y, X, 0). This is a more general 'catch-all' fact; Y can be bound to anything at all, equal to X or not. To correct the situation, a special predicate 'atomic' is needed together with the ability to express negative information.

d(Y,X,0) :– atomic(Y), not(Y=X).

atomic(Y) only succeeds if Y is a basic constant such as 4 or x, not mult(x,4). Expressing negative information is a more subtle problem. Prolog systems do have this ability, but it is included in various ways and as such is not part of the subset defined here. It is quite an easy matter to write a completely correct symbolic differentiator, that will also simplify its output, in full Prolog.

9.2 A formal definition

9.2.1 *Syntax*

Program:

$\gamma ::= \phi\ \psi \mid \psi$

Clause:

$\phi ::= \phi\ \phi \mid$

$\quad \pi :- \pi^{*}. \mid$ rule

$\quad \pi.$ fact

Predicate:

$\pi ::= \xi(\ \alpha^{+}\ ) \mid \xi$

Atom:

$\alpha ::= \nu \mid$ numeral

$\quad \xi \mid$ constant name

$\quad \Xi \mid$ variable name

$\quad \xi(\alpha^{+})$ function application

Query:

$\psi ::= ?\!-\ \pi^{*}.$

Prolog systems allow facts, rules and queries to be interleaved but it simplifies matters here if a program is restricted to a collection of rules and facts followed by one query.

9.2.2 *Semantic domains*

The variable names in a rule are *local* to that rule. The X in the definition of parent (§9.1) has no connection with the X in the definition of grandparent. The variables in a rule can be systematically changed without altering the meaning of the rule in any way. If a rule is recursive, new copies of the variable are used at each recursive invocation. There are several ways to define this in the semantics. The easiest is to map variables onto unique locations just before a clause is used. It is therefore convenient to create

ζ: **Locn ≡ Int**

Prolog is concerned with *symbolic computation*. The programmer might intend the constant-name 'charles' to denote some real individual '*charles*' but Prolog knows nothing of this.† Prolog computations are carried out in terms of the symbols occurring in the program; this is legitimized by results of Herbrand, see Nilsson [46] for example. It is therefore necessary to include the syntactic domains in the semantic domains and convenient to abuse the type system slightly:

α: **Value = Atom + Locn**
σ: **Store = Locn → Value**
ρ: **Env = Vars → Locn**
S = Int × Store

A state, **S**, is a free-storage counter and a store.

Continuation-semantics will be given, and an answer, **Ans**, is a list of values:

Ans = Value × Ans + {yes}

Queries that *fail* or are 'false' produce no output.

A *database* answers a simple query:

δ: **Database = Predicate → Database → Qcont → S → Ans**
θ: **Qcont = S → Ans**

A query continuation, **Qcont**, takes a computation state and produces an answer. A database has a database as a parameter to allow mutually recursive rules – the norm in Prolog. This is an alternative solution to the definition of mutual recursion discussed in §6.3.3.

A clause continuation, **CLcont**, is used in the processing of facts and rules:

κ: **CLcont = Database → Ans**

9.2.3 *Semantic equations*

The meaning of programs is given by four principal functions. **D** is responsible for the declaration of facts and rules and for setting up the database. **Q** processes queries. **P** organizes the execution of programs. **U** defines the unification process.

† The same can be said of the members of an enumerated type in Pascal.

$$\mathbf{P}: \mathbf{Program} \rightarrow \mathbf{Answer}$$
$$\mathbf{D}: \mathbf{Clause} \rightarrow \mathbf{Database} \rightarrow \mathbf{CLcont} \rightarrow \mathbf{Ans}$$
$$\mathbf{Q}: \mathbf{Query} \rightarrow \mathbf{Database} \rightarrow \mathbf{Qcont} \rightarrow \mathbf{S} \rightarrow \mathbf{Ans}$$
$$\mathbf{U}: \mathbf{Value}^2 \rightarrow \mathbf{Qcont} \rightarrow \mathbf{S} \rightarrow \mathbf{Ans}$$
$$\mathbf{P}[\![\ \phi\ \psi\ ]\!] = \mathbf{D}[\![\ \phi\ ]\!]\ \delta_0\ \mathbf{ask}$$
$$\text{where ask} = \lambda\delta\text{: } \mathbf{Q}[\![\ \psi'\ ]\!]\delta \text{ yes } \langle|\text{vars}|, \sigma_0\rangle$$
$$\text{and} \quad \text{vars} = \text{vars-in}[\![\psi]\!]$$
$$\text{and} \quad \rho = \lambda\xi\,.\,\text{index } \xi \text{ vars}$$
$$\text{and} \quad \psi' = \text{map } \rho\ [\![\psi]\!]$$

The result of a program is the result of declaring the facts and rules with a continuation which will ask the query. However, an environment ρ maps each identifier in the query onto a unique location and ψ' is the query with each variable replaced by the corresponding location.

$$\mathbf{Q}[\![\ \pi, \pi'\,.\ ]\!]\delta\theta\langle \text{f}, \sigma\rangle = \mathbf{Q}[\![\ \pi\,.\ ]\!]\delta\theta'\langle \text{f}, \sigma\rangle$$
$$\text{where } \theta' = \lambda\langle \text{f}', \sigma'\rangle.\mathbf{Q}[\![\ \pi'\,.\ ]\!]\delta\theta\langle \text{f}', \sigma'\rangle$$
$$\mathbf{Q}[\![\,.\,]\!]\delta\theta\langle \text{f}, \sigma\rangle = \theta\langle \text{f}, \sigma\rangle$$
$$\mathbf{Q}[\![\ \pi\,.\ ]\!]\delta\theta\langle \text{f}, \sigma\rangle = \delta[\![\pi]\!]\delta\theta\langle \text{f}, \sigma\rangle$$

To ask a query consisting of several predicates, ask the first part of the query with a continuation (for success) which asks the rest of the query. It is this clause that defines the left-to-right execution of rules. The empty query always succeeds and calls its continuation. To ask a query of one predicate, apply the database to the query.

$$\mathbf{D}[\![\ \phi\ \phi'\ ]\!]\delta\kappa = \mathbf{D}[\![\phi]\!]\delta\kappa'$$
$$\text{where } \kappa' = \lambda\delta'.\mathbf{D}[\![\phi']\!]\delta'\kappa$$
$$\mathbf{D}[\![\pi\,.\,]\!] = \mathbf{D}[\![\pi :\!-\,.\,]\!]$$
$$\mathbf{D}[\![\pi :\!- \pi^*.\,]\!]\delta\kappa = \kappa(\delta')$$
$$\text{where } \delta' = \lambda\pi'', \delta'', \theta, \langle \text{f}, \sigma\rangle.\text{append}(\delta[\![\pi'']\!]\delta''\theta\langle \text{f}, \sigma\rangle,$$
$$\mathbf{U}[\![\pi']\!][\![\pi'']\!]\theta'\langle \text{f}', \sigma'\rangle)$$
$$\text{where vars} = \text{vars-in } [\![\pi :\!- \pi^*]\!]$$
$$\text{and} \quad \text{f}' = \text{f} + |\text{vars}|$$
$$\text{and} \quad \rho = \lambda\xi\,.\,\text{f} + \text{index } \xi \text{ vars}$$
$$\text{and} \quad \pi' :\!- \pi^{*\prime} = \text{map } \rho\ [\![\pi :\!- \pi^*]\!]$$
$$\text{and} \quad \theta' = \mathbf{Q}[\![\pi^{*\prime}]\!]\theta$$

To declare a sequence of facts given a clause continuation to follow, declare the first fact with a continuation which declares the rest of the facts and then does the given continuation. To declare a basic fact, declare a rule with an empty right-hand side. To declare a single rule, apply the given continuation to a new database δ'. The new database firstly tries any queries in the old database, δ. It then attempts to unify (**U**) any query with the head of the given rule. Should they unify, the body of the rule will then be attempted. Since the body of the rule may use as yet undeclared facts, a database parameter δ'' is included to stand for the final total database. The (possible) results of the old database and the new rule are appended to form the answer; this defines the sequential search of the database.

9.2.4 *Unification*

The unification process is defined by **U**:

$$\begin{aligned}
&\mathbf{U}[\![v]\!][\![v']\!]\theta\langle \mathrm{f}, \sigma\rangle \\
&\quad = \theta\langle \mathrm{f}, \sigma\rangle \quad \text{if } v = v' \\
&\quad = \langle\,\rangle \qquad\quad \text{if } v \neq v' \\
&\mathbf{U}[\![\xi]\!][\![\xi']\!]\theta\langle \mathrm{f}, \sigma\rangle \\
&\quad = \theta\langle \mathrm{f}, \sigma\rangle \quad \text{if } \xi = \xi' \\
&\quad = \langle\,\rangle \qquad\quad \text{if } \xi \neq \xi' \\
&\mathbf{U}[\![\xi(\alpha^+)]\!][\![\xi'(\alpha^{+\prime})]\!]\theta\langle \mathrm{f}, \sigma\rangle \\
&\quad = \mathbf{U}[\![\alpha^+]\!][\![\alpha^{+\prime}]\!]\theta\langle \mathrm{f}, \sigma\rangle \quad \text{if } \xi = \xi' \\
&\quad = \langle\,\rangle \qquad\qquad\qquad\qquad\quad \text{if } \xi \neq \xi'
\end{aligned}$$

By an abuse of types, the last rule can define both the unification of functions and that of predicates.

$$\begin{aligned}
&\mathbf{U}[\![\alpha,\alpha^*]\!][\![\alpha',\alpha^{*\prime}]\!]\theta\langle \mathrm{f},\sigma\rangle \\
&\quad = \mathbf{U}[\![\alpha]\!][\![\alpha']\!]\theta'\langle \mathrm{f}, \sigma\rangle \\
&\qquad \text{where } \theta' = \lambda\langle \mathrm{f}', \sigma'\rangle.\,\mathbf{U}[\![\alpha^*]\!][\![\alpha^{*\prime}]\!]\theta\langle \mathrm{f}', \sigma'\rangle \\
&\mathbf{U}[\![\;]\!][\![\;]\!]\theta = \theta
\end{aligned}$$

The most interesting queries involve variables. However, by the time a query or fact gets to **U** it has been renamed so that all variables have been replaced by locations.

$$\begin{aligned}
&\mathbf{U}[\![\zeta]\!][\![\alpha]\!]\theta\langle \mathrm{f}, \sigma\rangle \\
&\quad = \mathbf{U}[\![\sigma(\zeta)]\!][\![\alpha]\!]\theta\langle \mathrm{f}, \sigma\rangle \quad \text{if } \sigma(\zeta) \neq \text{unset} \\
&\quad = \theta\langle \mathrm{f}, \sigma[\alpha/\zeta]\rangle \qquad\qquad \text{if } \sigma(\zeta) = \text{unset} \\
&\mathbf{U}[\![\alpha]\!][\![\zeta]\!] = \mathbf{U}[\![\zeta]\!][\![\alpha]\!]
\end{aligned}$$

If a location has a value, unify using that value. If a location is unset, to unify it with any value bind the location to the value in the store. Note, if two unset locations are unified, one will be bound to the other. If none of the above cases hold,

$$\mathbf{U}[\![\alpha]\!][\![\alpha']\!]\theta\langle \mathrm{f}, \sigma\rangle = \langle\,\rangle \text{ otherwise.}$$

There is a special start store and a start database:

$\sigma_0 = \lambda\zeta\,.\,\text{unset}$

$\delta_0 = \lambda\alpha, \delta, \theta, \langle f, \sigma\rangle.\ \text{if}\ \alpha = \text{write}(\alpha')\ \text{then}\ \langle \text{map}\ \sigma\ \alpha', \theta\langle f, \sigma\rangle\rangle\ \text{else}\ \langle\ \rangle$

Any further standard system predicates (routines) can be added to δ_0.

9.2.5 *Auxiliary functions*

There are a number of auxiliary functions used in the above definition:

map: **Store → Value → Value**

$\text{map}\ \sigma\ [\![v]\!] = v$

$\text{map}\ \sigma\ [\![\xi]\!] = \xi$

$\text{map}\ \sigma\ [\![\xi(\alpha^*)]\!] = \xi(\ \text{map}\ \sigma\ [\![\alpha^*]\!]\ )$

$\text{map}\ \sigma\ [\![\alpha, \alpha^*]\!] = \langle \text{map}\sigma[\![\alpha]\!], \text{map}\sigma[\![\alpha^*]\!]\rangle$

$\text{map}\ \sigma\ [\![\ ]\!] = \langle\ \rangle$

$\text{map}\ \sigma\ [\![\zeta]\!] = \zeta \quad \text{if}\ \sigma(\zeta) = \text{unset}$

$\qquad = \text{map}\ \sigma\ [\![\sigma(\zeta)]\!] \quad \text{otherwise}$

map converts any locations in an atom into their values, if known. There is another similar map:

map: **Env → Value → Value**

Yes is a continuation that returns the answer 'yes':

$\text{yes} = \lambda\ \sigma.\langle \text{yes}\rangle$: **Qcont**

it marks the end of a successful chain of deductions.

9.3 An Algol-68 translation

The definition of the Prolog subset can be translated into Algol-68 to give an interpreter. A simple parser can be written to return an Algol-68 data structure:

```
c syntactic domains: c
mod prog = struct(clist c, query q);
mode clist = ref clistnode,
        rule = struct(pred head, plist rhs);
mode clistnode = struct(clause h, clist t);
mode clause = union(pred c a fact c, rule);
mode applic = struct(alfa id, alist args);   c f(x,g(,y))c
mode plist = ref plistnode;
mode plistnode = struct(pred h, plist t);
mode pred = union(applic, alfa);   c odd(7). or p. c
```

```
mode query = plist;
mode alist = ref alistnode;
mode alistnode = struct(atom h, alist t);
mode name = struct(int tag, alfa id);   c ⟨ident, fred⟩ or ⟨varsy, FRED⟩
mode atom = union(int, name, applic,   c numeral | ident | IDENT | f(arg
                  locn c NB. locn for value not for atom c);
```

The semantic domains also become **modes**:

```
mode value = atom,
     vlist = alist;
mode ans = ref anscell;
mode anscell = struct(value h, ans t);
mode locn = struct(int l, dont care);
mode env = proc(alfa)locn,
     store = proc(locn)value;
mode database = proc(pred, database, qcont, int, store)ans;
mode qcont = proc(int, store)ans;
mode clcont = proc(database)ans;
```

The auxiliary functions are straightforward although the fact that Algol-68 is not polymorphic makes for some duplication.

```
qcont yes = (int l, store s)ans:
  heap anscell := (name(ident, alfa("yes*******")),
                   nil);

database start d = (pred p, database d, qcont c, int l, store s)ans:
  ( proc map s val = (value v)value:
      case v in
      (locn l): if not set(s(l)) then v else map s val(s(l)) fi,
      (applic f): applic(id of f, map s list(args of f))
      out v
      esac;
    proc map s list = (vlist l)vlist:
      if l is nil
        then nil
        else heap alistnode := (map s val(h of l), map s list(t of l))
      fi;
```

```
case p in
   (alfa x): nil,
   (applic f): if id of f=alfa("write      ")
                  then heap anscell := (map s val(h of args of f),
                                                  c(l, s))
                  else nil
               fi
esac
);
store start s=(locn ln)value: unset;
```

P is the main driver routine:

```
proc P=(prog p)ans:
   ( clcont ask=(database d)ans:
        ( alfas vars=vars in plist(q of p);
          int n vars=length(vars);
          env e=(alfa a)locn: (index(a, vars), 0);
          Q(map e plist(e, q of p), d, yes, n vars, start s)
        );
     D(c of p, start d, ask)
   );
```

Q processes queries:

```
proc Q=(query q, database d, qcont c, int l, store s)ans:
   if q is nil
     then c(l, s)
     else qcont ask tail=(int l, store s)ans: Q(t of q, d, c, l, s);
          d(h of q, d, ask tail, l, s)
   fi;
```

D declares facts and rules:

```
proc D=(union(clist, clause) f, database d, clcont k) ans:
   case f in
   (clist f): if f is nil
                 then k(d)
                 else clcont do tail=(database d)ans: D(t of f,d,k);
                         D(h of f, d, do tail)
              fi;
   (clause f):
      case f in
      (pred p): D( rule(p, nil), d, k),
```

```
     (rule r): ( c head :- rhs.   e.g. p :- q, r.   c
                database new d = (pred p, database final d,
                                          qcont c, int l, store s)ans:
                  (alfas vars = vars in clause(f);
                  int n vars = length(vars);
                  int l2 = l + n vars;
                  store s2 = (locn ln)value:
                     if l of ln > l then unset else s(ln) fi;
                  env e = (alfa a)locn: (index(a, vars) + 1, 0);
                  qcont ask body = (int l, store s) ans:
                        Q(map e plist(e, rhs of r), final d, c, l, s);
                  append( d(p, final d, c, l, s),
                          U pred(map e pred(e, head of r), p,
                                                  ask body, l2, s2))
                  )c new d c;
                k(new d)
               )
     esac
   esac;
```

Different versions of U are needed for unifying predicates, values and lists:

```
  proc U pred = (pred a, b, qcont c, int l, store s)ans:
     case a in
     (alfa pa): case b in
                (alfa pb): if pa = pb then c(l, s) else nil fi
                out nil
                esac,
     (applic fa): case b in
                 (applic fb): if id of fa = id of fb
                                  then U list(args of fa, args of fb, c, l, s)
                                  else nil
                              fi
                 out nil
                 esac
     esac;
  proc U list = (vlist a, q, qcont c, int l, store s)ans:
     if (a is nil) or (q is nil)
       then if a is q then c(l, s) else nil fi
       else qcont do tail = (int l, store s)ans:
                U list(t of a, t of q, c, l, s);
            U(h of a, h of q, do tail, l, s)
     fi;
```

```
proc U=(value a, q, qcont c, int l, store s)ans:
   ( proc update=(locn x, value v)ans:
        if not set(s(x))
           then proc new s=(locn x2)value:
                      if x=x2 then v else s(x2) fi;
                c(l, new s)
           else U(s(x), v, c, l, s)
        fi;
     case q in
     (name nq): c must be a const-ident not a VAR c
                case a in
                (locn la): update(la, q),
                (name na): if id of nq=id of na then c(l, s) else nil fi
                out nil
                esac,
     (locn lq): update(lq, a),
     (int nq): case a in
               (locn la): update(la, q),
               (int na): if nq=na then c(l, s) else nil fi
               out nil
               esac,
     (applic fq): case a in
                (locn la): update(la, q),
                (applic fa): if id of fq=id of fa
                                then U list(args of fq, args of fa, c, l, s)
                                else nil
                             fi;
                out nil
                esac
     esac
   ) c U c;
```

When the auxiliary functions are added, the call

show(**P**(parser))

parses and executes a program and displays the result. Note that this interpreter does not define programs that do not terminate.

9.4 Exercises

1. Define the relationships sibling, brother, sister, aunt and uncle in Prolog. Beware of circular definitions.

2. Extend the semantics to include negation:

   Predicate:

   π ::= **not** π | . . .

   not π succeeds exactly when π fails. (This is a common implementation of negation but it is not correct if π contains unbound variables.)

3. Extend the semantics to allow queries to be interleaved with clauses. A query may only 'use' those clauses that appear prior to the query.

4. **Project:** implement a semantics of Prolog in a suitable programming language, *or* modify a given implementation to include some of the above.

10
Miscellaneous

The preceding chapters introduced the main ideas in the use of denotational semantics to define sequential programming languages. This chapter touches on some wider issues, firstly on executing definitions which has been implicit in preceding chapters, and then on concurrency which has not been examined but is an important research area.

10.1 Interpreters and compiler-compilers

λ-Notation is itself capable of formal definition. This has not been done here in the interests of space and because there are advantages in using it somewhat informally! λ-Notation is also capable of being implemented in various ways to allow denotational definitions to be run to give implementations. Mosses' SIS [41] is a system for interpreting definitions to give interpreters. The functional language ML [20]† has essentially all the power of λ-notation and a definition written in ML can be compiled (or interpreted) to give an interpreter. This allows definitions to be tested very easily. Paulson [49], Raskovsky [50], Sethi [57] and others [28] have investigated compiling λ-notation into compilers. Hence the compiler for λ-notation would be a true compiler-compiler. Paulson claims a system which produces good code for significant programming languages.

If **DS** is the language of denotational semantics, δ is a particular definition of some programming language, δ: **DS**, π is a program and ι is some input for the program then

$$\mathbf{C_1 : DS \times Prog \times Input \to Ans}$$
$$\mathbf{C}[\![\delta\ \pi\ \iota]\!]$$

can describe interpreting δ and π on ι.

† Although ML does not use normal-order evaluation.

Alternatively,

$$\mathbf{C}_2\mathbf{: DS \rightarrow Prog \times Input \rightarrow Ans}$$
$$(\mathbf{C}_2[\![\delta]\!])[\![\pi\ \iota]\!]$$

is the result of compiling the definition δ to make an interpreter $\mathbf{C}_2[\![\delta]\!]$ and then using that to run π on ι. This has been used implicitly in previous chapters where a definition was written in Pascal or Algol-68 instead of **DS** and then compiled to give an interpreter.

To use δ to generate a compiler $\mathbf{C}_3[\![\delta]\!]$ and then to compile π and finally run it:

$$\mathbf{C}_3\mathbf{: DS \rightarrow Prog \rightarrow Input \rightarrow Ans}$$
$$((\mathbf{C}_3[\![\delta]\!])[\![\pi]\!])[\![\iota]\!]$$

$\mathbf{C}_3$ can be realized in two steps. δ can be treated as a method of translating **Prog** into λ-calculus, Λ.

$$\text{example: } \mathbf{C}_4[\![\delta_{\mathrm{Ch\,5}}]\!][\![\ \mathrm{x} := 7\ ]\!] = \lambda\sigma\,.\,\sigma[7/\mathrm{x}]$$
$$\mathbf{C}_4\mathbf{: DS \rightarrow Prog \rightarrow} \Lambda$$

Given a compiler $\mathrm{L}: \Lambda \rightarrow \mathbf{Input} \rightarrow \mathbf{Ans}$ for Λ,

$$\mathbf{C}_3[\![\delta]\!] \equiv \mathrm{L} \circ (\mathbf{C}_4[\![\delta]\!])\mathbf{: Prog \rightarrow Input \rightarrow Ans}$$

Note that the $\mathbf{C}_i$ are different semantics for the same (syntactic) language **DS**.

Ershov [16] and Jones and Tofte [30] have examined many interesting questions in compiler generation along the lines above, particularly what sort of language a compiler-compiler might be written in and how it might generate itself!

10.2 Concurrency

Concurrent programming languages have not been examined at all in this book. There are various attempts to describe concurrency formally. The major problems are shared storage, timing and scheduling.

One rule of denotational semantics is that the semantics of a construction in a language is given in terms of its components, and possibly some parameters, only. With shared storage, however, the state of a process might change without warning owing to the action of other processes. Processes are intended to run asynchronously which means that many possible outcomes are possible in a given computation. This is implemented by a process running when resources are available. A semantics should not include a detailed model of the computer, its peripherals, the real world and anything else that might affect process scheduling but should address questions of *fairness* and deadlock.

In the formal definition of Ada by Bjorner, Oest and others [5], the static and sequential semantics are given in a denotational style. The parallel parts of the language are described by a separate, more operational model.

In formal treatments of concurrency, there is a trend to omit shared storage and restrict interaction of processes to communication. Hoare's Communicating Sequential Processes (CSP) [25, 26] is a language where processes may interact only via disciplined message passing. As such, its semantics are more elegant.

Milner's Calculus of Communicating Systems (CCS) [38] is a formalism for describing concurrent processes. There are experimental implementations of CCS [39] to form a concurrent functional language. A process without shared memory has much in common with a function. To write to a process, send a write message, or parameter, and receive an acknowledgement. To read, send a read request and receive some data. The difference is that time may pass between the request, or call, and the acknowledgement, or result.

Appendix: Interpreter for Chapter 5

```
program ch5(input, output);

label 99;

type  {lexical objects}
      alfa = packed array [1..10] of char;
      symbol = (plussy, minussy, timessy, oversy,
                eqsy, nesy, ltsy, lesy, gtsy, gesy,
                ident, numeral,
                ifsy, thensy, elsesy, whilesy, dosy,
                beginsy, endsy, skipsy,
                semisy, becomessy, open, close, stopsy);

      {syntactic domains}
      exptype = (bexp, uexp, varr, int);
      opr     = (plus, minus, times, over,
                 eq, ne, lt, le, gt, ge, neg);
      cmdtype = (assign, semi, ifstat, whiles, skip);

      exp = ↑ enode;
      enode = record case tag:exptype of
                 bexp    :(o:opr; left, right:exp);
                 uexp    :(u:opr; son:exp);
                 varr    :(id:alfa);
                 int     :(i:integer);
              end;

      cmd = ↑ cnode;
      cnode = record case tag:cmdtype of
                 assign  :(id:alfa; e:exp);
                 semi    :(left,right:cmd);
                 ifstat  :(b:exp; gtrue,gfalse:cmd);
                 whiles  :(bw:exp; g:cmd);
                 skip    :()
              end;

      {semantic domains}
      Value = integer;

      State = ↑ avar;
      avar  = record ident:alfa;
                     v:Value;
                     next:State
              end;

var lineno:integer;
    ch : char    {current character};
    sy : symbol {current symbol class};
    word : alfa {current keyword, identifier or operator};
    n : integer {value of current numeral};
```

```
{-----------------------------------------------------------lexical-----}
procedure error(a:alfa);
begin writeln;
      writeln(' error:', a,' ch=<',ch,'> word=<',word,'> n=',n:1);
      goto 99
end;

function nextch:char;
   var ch:char;
begin if eof then error('prem'' eof ')
      else if eoln then
      begin readln; writeln;
            lineno:=lineno+1; write(lineno:4,':');
            nextch:='
      end
      else begin read(ch); write(ch); nextch:=ch
           end
end;

procedure insymbol;
   var l:integer; ch2:char;
begin while ch=' ' do ch:=nextch;
      if ch in ['a'..'z','A'..'Z'] then
      begin l:=0; word:='          ';
            while ch in ['a'..'z','A'..'Z','0'..'9'] do
            begin l:=l+1;
                  if l<=10 then word[l]:=ch;
                  ch:=nextch
            end;
                 if word = 'begin     ' then sy:=beginsy
            else if word = 'end       ' then sy:=endsy
            else if word = 'if        ' then sy:=ifsy
            else if word = 'then      ' then sy:=thensy
            else if word = 'else      ' then sy:=elsesy
            else if word = 'while     ' then sy:=whilesy
            else if word = 'do        ' then sy:=dosy
            else if word = 'skip      ' then sy:=skipsy
            else sy:= ident
      end
      else if ch in ['0'..'9'] then
      begin n:=0;
            while ch in ['0'..'9'] do
            begin n:=n*10+ord(ch)-ord('0');
                  ch:=nextch
            end;
            sy:=numeral
      end
      else if ch in ['+', '-', '*', '/', '=', '(', ')', ';', '.'] then
      begin case ch of
               '+': sy:=plussy;
               '-': sy:=minussy;
               '*': sy:=timessy;
               '/': sy:=oversy;
```

```
                '=': sy:=eqsy;
                '(': sy:=open;
                ')': sy:=close;
                ';': sy:=semisy;
                '.': sy:=stopsy
             end;
             ch:=nextch
       end
       else if ch in ['<', '>', ':'] then
       begin ch2:=ch; ch:=nextch;
             case ch2 of
                '<': if ch='=' then sy:=lesy
                     else if ch='>' then sy:=nesy else sy:=ltsy;
                '>': if ch='=' then sy:=gesy else sy:=gtsy;
                ':': if ch='=' then sy:=becomessy
                     else error('no = in :=')
             end;
             if sy in [lesy,nesy,gesy,becomessy]  then ch:=nextch
       end else error('insymbol  ')
end {insymbol};

procedure check(s:symbol; chs:alfa);
   var m:alfa;
begin if sy=s then insymbol
      else begin m:='chck(    )';
                 m[6]:=chs[1]; m[7]:=chs[2]; m[8]:=chs[3];
                 m[9]:=chs[4]; error(m)
           end
end;

function nextsymis(s:symbol):boolean;
begin nextsymis:=true;
      if sy=s then insymbol else nextsymis:=false
end;

function consexp(t:exptype; f:opr; e1,e2:exp):exp;
   var e:exp;
begin new(e); consexp:=e;
      with e↑ do
      begin tag := t; o:=f;
            left:=e1; right:=e2
      end
end;

function conscmd(t:cmdtype; ctrle:exp; g1,g2:cmd):cmd;
   var c:cmd;
begin new(c); conscmd:=c;
      with c↑ do
      begin tag:=t;
            case t of
               assign: error('cons cmd  ');
               semi:   begin left:=g1; right:=g2 end;
               ifstat: begin b:=ctrle; gtrue:=g1; gfalse:=g2 end;
```

```
          whiles: begin bw:=ctrle;g:=gl end;
          skip:
        end
    end
end;
{--------------------------------------------------------parser--------------}
function parser:cmd;

  function pexp:exp;
    var e:exp; o:opr;

    function pexp1:exp;
      var e:exp; o:opr;

      function pexp2:exp;
        var e:exp; o:opr;

        function pexp3:exp;
          var e:exp;
        begin if sy=open then
            begin insymbol;
                e:=pexp;
                check(close, ')          ')
            end
            else if sy=minussy then
            begin insymbol;
                e:=consexp(uexp, neg, pexp3, nil)
            end
            else if sy=ident then
            begin new(e);
                with e↑ do
                begin tag:=varr; id:=word
                end;
                insymbol
            end
            else if sy=numeral then
            begin new(e);
                with e↑ do
                begin tag:=int; i:=n
                end;
                insymbol
            end
            else error('pexp3     ');
            pexp3:=e
        end {pexp3};

      begin {pexp2}
        e:=pexp3;
        while sy in [timessy,oversy] do
        begin if sy=timessy then o:=times
            else o:=over;
            insymbol;
            e:=consexp(bexp, o, e, pexp3)
```

```
      end;
      pexp2:=e
    end {pexp2};

  begin {pexp1}
    e:=pexp2;
    while sy in [plussy,minussy] do
    begin if sy=plussy then o:=plus
        else o:=minus;
        insymbol;
        e:=consexp(bexp, o, e, pexp2)
    end;
    pexp1:=e
  end {pexp1};

begin {pexp}
  e:=pexp1;
  if sy in [eqsy .. gesy] then
  begin case sy of
          eqsy: o:=eq; nesy: o:=ne;
          ltsy: o:=lt; lesy: o:=le;
          gtsy: o:=gt; gesy: o:=ge
      end;
      insymbol;
      e:=consexp(bexp, o, e, pexp1)
  end;
  pexp:=e
end {pexp};

function pcmd:cmd;
  var c:cmd;
      x:alfa;

      function ifcmd:cmd;
        var e:exp; g1:cmd;
      begin e:=pexp;
          check(thensy, 'then      '); g1:=pcmd;
          check(elsesy, 'else      ');
          ifcmd:=conscmd(ifstat,e,g1,pcmd)
      end {ifcmd};

      function whilecmd:cmd;
        var e:exp;
      begin e:=pexp; check(dosy, 'do        ');
          whilecmd:=conscmd(whiles, e, pcmd,nil)
      end;

begin if sy=ident then
    begin x:=word;
        insymbol; check(becomessy, ':=        ');
        new(c);
        with c↑ do  {x:=rhs}
        begin tag:=assign; id:=x; e:=pexp
```

```
            end
        end
        else if nextsymis(ifsy) then
            c:=ifcmd
        else if nextsymis(whilesy) then
            c:=whilecmd
        else if nextsymis(beginsy) then
        begin c:=pcmd;
            while nextsymis(semisy) do
                c:=conscmd(semi, nil, c, pcmd);
            check(endsy, 'end      ')
        end
        else if nextsymis(skipsy) then
           c:=conscmd(skip, nil,nil,nil)
        else error('parse cmd ');
        pcmd := c
   end {pcmd};

begin {parser}
   parser:=pcmd;
   if sy<>stopsy then error('no .      ')
end {parser};
{----------------------------------------------------------------semantics--}
procedure display(s:State);
begin if s=nil then writeln(' finish')
      else begin writeln(s↑.ident,'=',s↑.v:3); display(s↑.next)
           end
end;

function undefined:Value;
{not a function in the semantics; a fn here to get side-effect of stop}
begin error('run:undef ') end;

function update(s:State; id:alfa; val:Value):State;
             { : State x Ide x Value -> State }
   var p:State;
begin new(p); p↑.next:=s; update:=p;
      p↑.ident:=id; p↑.v:=val
end;

function applyState(s:State; id:alfa):Value;
begin if s=nil then applyState:=undefined
      else if s↑.ident = id then applyState:=s↑.v
      else applyState:=applyState(s↑.next, id)
end;

function E(e:exp; s:State):Value; {: exp x State -> Value }
   function O(o:opr; v1, v2 :Value):Value;
   begin case o of
            plus: O:=v1+v2;
            minus:O:=v1-v2;
            times:O:=v1*v2;
            over: O:=v1 div v2;
```

```
            eq:    O:=ord(v1=v2);
            ne:    O:=ord(v1<>v2);
            lt:    O:=ord(v1<v2);
            le:    O:=ord(v1<=v2);
            gt:    O:=ord(v1>v2);
            ge:    O:=ord(v1>=v2)
         end {case}
   end {O};

begin {E}
   case e↑.tag of
      varr:   E:=applyState(s, e↑.id);
      int:    E:=e↑.i;
      uexp:   E:= - E(e↑.son, s) {- only unary op};
      bexp:   E:= O( e↑.o, E(e↑.left, s), E(e↑.right,s))
   end {case}
end {E};

function C(g:cmd; s:State):State; {: cmd x State -> State}
begin {Main interpreter routine}
   case g↑.tag of
      assign:   C:=update(s, g↑.id, E(g↑.e, s));
      semi:     C:=C(g↑.right, C(g↑.left, s));
      ifstat:   if E(g↑.b,s)=1 then C:=C(g↑.gtrue,s)
                               else C:=C(g↑.gfalse,s);
      whiles:   if E(g↑.bw,s)=1 then C:=C(g, C(g↑.g,s))
                                else C:=s;
      skip:     C:=s
   end {case}
end {C};
{-----------------------------------------------------------------main---}
begin
   writeln(' A Simple Language, L.Allison U.W.A.');
   lineno:=1; write(lineno:4, ':');
   word:='-starting-'; n:=0; ch:=nextch; insymbol;

   display( C(parser, {startState=}nil ) );
   99: {fin}
end.
```

References

[1] *Tenth Annual ACM Symposium on the Principles of Programming Languages*. ACM, Jan. 1983.

[2] *Eleventh Annual ACM Symposium on the Principles of Programming Languages*. ACM, Jan. 1984.

[3] L. Allison. Programming denotational semantics. *BCJ* **26**, No. 2, 164–74, Feb. 1983.

[4] E. A. Ashcroft and W. W. Wadge. Ɽ for semantics. *ACM TOPLAS* **4**, No. 2, 283–94, April 1982.

[5] D. Bjorner and O. N. Oest (eds.). *Towards a Formal Description of Ada*. Springer-Verlag LNCS 98, 1980.

[6] W. H. Burge. *Recursive Programming Techniques*. Addison-Wesley, 1975.

[7] A. Church. *The Calculi of λ-Conversion*. Annals of Mathematical Studies 6. Princeton UP, 1951.

[8] J. C. Cleaveland and R. C. Uzgalis. *Grammars for Programming Languages*. Elsevier North-Holland, 1977.

[9] W. F. Clocksin and C. S. Mellish. *Programming in Prolog*. Springer-Verlag, 1981.

[10] M. Coppo. On the semantics of polymorphism. *Acta Informatica* **20**, No. 2, 159–70, Nov. 1983.

[11] P. Cousot and R. Cousot. Abstract interpretation: a unified lattice model for static analysis of programs by construction or approximation of fixed-points. In *Fourth Annual ACM Symposium on the Principles of Programming Languages*. ACM, Jan. 1977.

[12] H. B. Curry. Some philosophical aspects of combinatory logic. In *The Kleene Symposium*, 1978, J. Barwise, H. J. Keisler and K. Kunnen (eds.), pp. 85–101. North-Holland, 1980.

[13] E. W. Dijkstra. *A Discipline of Programming*. Prentice-Hall, 1976.

[14] J. E. Donahue. *Complementary Definitions of Programming Language Semantics*. Springer-Verlag LNCS 42, 1976.

[15] D. R. Dowty, R. E. Wall and S. Peters. *Introduction to Montague Semantics*. D. Reidel, 1981.

[16] A. P. Ershov. Mixed computation: potential applications and problems for study. *Theoretical Computer Science* **18**, 41–67, 1982.

[17] R. W. Floyd. Assigning meaning to programs. In *Proceedings of the Symposium in Applied Mathematics*. Mathematical Aspects of Computer Science 19, 1967.

[18] S. Fortune, D. Leivant and M. O'Donnell. The expressiveness of simple and second-order type structures. *JACM* **30**, No. 1, 151–85, Jan. 1985.

[19] M. P. Georgeff and G. Eddy. Functional Pascal: an extension of Pascal to higher-order functions. Monash University TR27, Dec. 1982.

[20] M. J. C. Gordon, R. Milner and C. Wadsworth. *Edinburgh LCF*. Springer-Verlag LNCS 78, 1979.
[21] M. J. C. Gordon. *The Denotational Description of Programming Languages*. Springer-Verlag, 1979.
[22] P. Henderson. *Functional Programming: Application and Implementation*. Prentice-Hall, 1980.
[23] P. Henderson and J. H. Morris. A lazy evaluator. In *Third Annual ACM Symposium on the Principles of Programming Languages*, pp. 95–103. ACM, 1976.
[24] C. A. R. Hoare. An axiomatic basis for computer programming. *CACM* **12**, No. 10, 576–80, Oct. 1969.
[25] C. A. R. Hoare. Communicating sequential processes. *CACM* **21**, No. 8, 666–77, Aug. 1978.
[26] C. A. R. Hoare. Notes on CSP. Preprint 83/4 Programming Research Group, Oxford University, March 1983.
[27] K. E. Iverson. *A Programming Language*. Wiley, 1962.
[28] N. D. Jones (ed.). *Semantics-Directed Compiler Generation*. Springer-Verlag LNCS 94, 1980.
[29] N. D. Jones and A. M. Mycroft. Stepwise development of operational and denotational semantics for Prolog. Draft, April 1983, Copenhagen/Edinburgh Universities.
[30] N. D. Jones and M. Tofte. *Towards a Theory of Compiler Generation*. Datalogisk Institut, Copenhagen, Denmark, May 1984.
[31] G. Khan, D. B. MacQueen and G. Plotkin (eds.). *Semantics of Data Types*. Springer-Verlag LNCS 173, 1984.
[32] R. Kowalski. Algorithm = Logic + Control. *CACM* **22**, No. 7, 424–35, July 1979.
[33] D. MacQueen and G. Plotkin. An ideal model for recursive polymorphic types. In [2].
[34] J. McCarthy *et al. Lisp 1.5 Programmer's Manual*. MIT Press, 1962.
[35] A. D. McGettrick. *The Definition of Programming Languages*. Cambridge Computer Science Texts 11. CUP, 1980.
[36] R. Milne and C. Strachey. *A Theory of Programming Language Semantics* (2 vols.). Chapman and Hall, 1976.
[37] R. Milner. A theory of type polymorphism in programming. *Jnl Computer and System Science* **17**, 348–75, 1978.
[38] R. Milner. *A Calculus of Communicating Systems*. Springer-Verlag LNCS 92, 1980.
[39] K. Mitchell. *A User's Guide to PFL*. Edinburgh University, 1983.
[40] P. Mosses. The mathematical semantics of Algol 60. PRG-12. Oxford University Programming Research Group, 1974.
[41] P. Mosses. *SIS – Semantics Implementation System, Reference Manual and User's Guide*. University of Aarhus, Denmark, 1979.
[42] A. Mycroft. Call by need = call by value + conditional. Department of Computer Science, Edinburgh, CSR-78-81.
[43] L. Naish. *MU-Prolog 2.4 Reference Manual*. Melbourne University, July 1982.
[44] P. Naur (ed.). *Revised Report on the Algorithmic Language Algol 60*. International Federation of Information Processing, 1960.
[45] T. Nicholson and N. Foo. *A Denotational Semantics for Prolog*. Basser Department of Computer Science, University of Sydney, Australia, 1985.
[46] N. J. Nilsson. *Problem-Solving Methods in Artificial Intelligence*. McGraw-Hill, 1971.

[47] F. G. Pagan. Algol-68 as a metalanguage for denotational semantics. *BCJ* **22**, No. 1, 63–6, Feb. 1979.

[48] F. G. Pagan. *Formal Specifications of Programming Languages*. Prentice-Hall, 1981.

[49] L. C. Paulson. A compiler generator for semantic grammars (Ph.D. thesis). Stanford, 1982.

[50] M. R. Raskovsky. Denotational-semantics as a specification of code generators. In *Proceedings of the* 1982 *Sigplan Symposium on Compiler Construction*, p. 230. ACM, 1982.

[51] J. C. Reynolds. Towards a theory of type structure. In *Conference on Programming*, pp. 408–25. Springer-Verlag LNCS 19, 1974.

[52] M. Richards. BCPL: a tool for compiler writing and system programming. *Proceedings of the Spring Joint Computer Conference* **34**, 557–66, 1969.

[53] J. A. Robinson. A machine-oriented logic based on the resolution principle. *JACM* **12**, 23–41, 1965.

[54] D. Scott and C. Strachey. Towards a mathematical semantics for computer languages. PRG-6. Oxford University Programming Research Group, 1971.

[55] D. Scott. Continuous lattices. PRG-7. Oxford University Programming Research Group, 1971.

[56] D. Scott. Data types as lattices. *SIAM J. Comput.* **5**, No. 3, 522–87, Sept. 1976.

[57] R. Sethi. Control-flow aspects of semantics directed compiling. In *Proceedings of the* 1982 *Sigplan Symposium on Compiler Construction*, p. 245. ACM, 1982.

[58] J. E. Stoy. *Denotational Semantics: the Scott–Strachey Approach to Programming Language Theory*. MIT Press, 1977.

[59] C. Strachey. Towards a formal semantics. In *Formal Language Description Languages*, T. B. Steel (ed.), pp. 198–220. North-Holland, 1966.

[60] C. Strachey. The varieties of programming languages. PRG-10. Oxford University Programming Research Group, 1973.

[61] C. Strachey and C. P. Wadsworth. Continuations, a mathematical semantics for handling full jumps. PRG-11. Oxford University Programming Research Group, 1974.

[62] R. D. Tennent. The denotational semantics of programming languages. *CACM* **19**, No. 8, 437–53, Aug. 1976.

[63] R. D. Tennent. *A Denotational Definition of the Programming Language Pascal*. Oxford University Programming Research Group, 1978.

[64] D. A. Turner. A new implementation technique for applicative languages. *Software Practice and Experience* **9**, 31–49, 1979.

[65] A. van Wijngaarden *et al. Revised Report on the Algorithmic Language Algol* 68. Springer-Verlag, 1976.

[66] C. P. Wadsworth. Semantics and pragmatics of the λ-calculus (Ph.D. thesis). Oxford University, 1971.

Index of definitions

Subject index